Faith & Religion

Series Editor: Cara Acred

Volume 285

Independence Educational Publishers

First published by Independence Educational Publishers

The Studio, High Green

Great Shelford

Cambridge CB22 5EG

England

© Independence 2015

Photocopy licence

The material in this book is protected by copyright. However, the

purchaser is free to make multiple copies of particular articles for instructional

purposes for immediate use within the purchasing institution.

Making copies of the entire book is not permitted.

British Library Cataloguing in Publication Data

Faith & religion. -- (Issues ; 285)

1. Great Britain--Religion--21st century. 2. Great

Britain--Religious life and customs.

I. Series II. Acred, Cara editor.

200.9'41-dc23

ISBN-13: 9781861687173

Printed in Great Britain
Zenith Print Group

Contents

Introduction

Faith & Religion is Volume 285 in the **ISSUES** series. The aim of the series is to offer current, diverse information about important issues in our world, from a UK perspective.

ABOUT FAITH & RELIGION

Today, issues of faith and religion are becoming more and more complex. Increasingly fewer people in the UK consider themselves to be religious, with 65% of young people saying they do not believe in a God. This book considers the many debates surrounding religion, both in the UK and globally, including questions about fasting and Ramadan, Britain's first 'atheist church' and the link between schools and religious education.

OUR SOURCES

Titles in the **ISSUES** series are designed to function as educational resource books, providing a balanced overview of a specific subject.

The information in our books is comprised of facts, articles and opinions from many different sources, including:

⇨ Newspaper reports and opinion pieces

⇨ Website factsheets

⇨ Magazine and journal articles

⇨ Statistics and surveys

⇨ Government reports

⇨ Literature from special interest groups

A NOTE ON CRITICAL EVALUATION

Because the information reprinted here is from a number of different sources, readers should bear in mind the origin of the text and whether the source is likely to have a particular bias when presenting information (or when conducting their research). It is hoped that, as you read about the many aspects of the issues explored in this book, you will critically evaluate the information presented.

It is important that you decide whether you are being presented with facts or opinions. Does the writer give a biased or unbiased report? If an opinion is being expressed, do you agree with the writer? Is there potential bias to the 'facts' or statistics behind an article?

ASSIGNMENTS

In the back of this book, you will find a selection of assignments designed to help you engage with the articles you have been reading and to explore your own opinions. Some tasks will take longer than others and there is a mixture of design, writing and research-based activities that you can complete alone or in a group.

FURTHER RESEARCH

At the end of each article we have listed its source and a website that you can visit if you would like to conduct your own research. Please remember to critically evaluate any sources that you consult and consider whether the information you are viewing is accurate and unbiased.

Useful weblinks

www.acnuk.org

www.biblesociety.org.uk

www.catholicherald.co.uk

www.channel4.com

www.christiantoday.com

www.theconversation.com

www.debatewise.org

www.enar-eu.org

www.equalityhumanrights.com

www.faithdebates.org.uk

http://freethoughtreport.com

www.theguardian.com

humanism.org.uk

www.independent.co.uk

www.ipsos-mori-generations.com

www.onreligion.co.uk

www.pewforum.org

www.pressassociation.com

www.secularism.org.uk

www.telegraph.co.uk

www.theosthinktank.co.uk

yougov.co.uk

Religion and belief: some surveys and statistics

Numerous surveys indicate that the proportion of individuals who do not hold religious beliefs is steadily increasing.

Religions and beliefs are notoriously difficult to measure, as they are not fixed or innate, and therefore any poll should be primarily treated as an indication of beliefs rather than a concrete measure.

However, one of the foremost respected measures of religious attitudes is the annual *British Social Attitudes Survey*, further details of the latest report may be found on NatCen's website.

Surveys and polls on religion and belief in the United Kingdom

Census data

The English and Welsh Census uses the highly leading question 'What is your religion?' By assuming that all participants hold a religious belief, the question captures some kind of loose cultural affiliation, and as a result over in 2001 70% of the population responded 'Christian'; a far higher percentage than nearly every other significant survey or poll on religious belief in the past decade.

The Office for National Statistics understands the religion question to be a proxy question for ethnicity. This is in order to capture the Jewish and Sikh populations, both of which are captured under race legislation but are not included in the ethnicity category in the Census, as they should be, rather than the religion category. The result is that a very loose, cultural affiliation is 'measured' by the Census in terms of religion or belief, with particular over-

inflation of the Christian figure, and an undercounting of the non-religious population. As a result, the Census data on religion is most definitely not suitable for use by employers or service providers

2011 Census

According to the 2011 UK Census, those of no religion are the second largest belief group, about three and a half times as many as all the non-Christian religions put together – at 26.13% of the population. 16,038,229 people said they had 'no religion' with a further 4,406,032 (7.18%) not stating a religion. 58.81% described their religion as Christian and 7.88% as some non-Christian religion. This represented a massive change from the 2001 Census, where 15.5% of the population recorded having no religion, and 72% of the population reported being Christian.

However, in a poll conducted by YouGov in March 2011 on behalf of the BHA, when asked the Census question 'What is your religion?', 61% of people in England and Wales ticked a religious box (53.48% Christian and 7.22% other) while 39% ticked 'No religion'. When the same sample was asked the follow-up question 'Are you religious?', only 29% of the same people said 'Yes' while 65% said 'No', meaning over half of those whom the Census would count as having a religion said they were not religious.

Less than half (48%) of those who ticked 'Christian' said they believed that Jesus Christ was a real person who died and came back to life and was the son of God.

Asked when they had last attended a place of worship for religious reasons, most people in England and Wales (63%) had not attended in the past

year: 43% of people last attended over a year ago and 20% of people had never attended. Only 9% of people reported having attended a place of worship within the last week.

The Humanist Society of Scotland commissioned a separate poll asking the Scottish Census question, 'What religion, religious denomination or body do you belong to?'. In response, 42% of the adult population in Scotland said 'None'.

When asked 'Are you religious?', 56% of the same sample said they were not and only 35% said they were.

Other surveys and polls on religion and belief in the UK

In the UK, the percentage of the population which describes itself as belonging to no religion has risen from 31.4% to 50.6% between 1983 and 2013 according to the *British Social Attitudes Survey*'s 31st report issued in 2014. Among people aged between 15 and 24, the incidence of religious affiliation is only 30.7%. It is only amongst the over-55s that the majority of respondents are religious.

Conversely, the report found that only 41.7% of people in the UK identify as Christians compared to 49.9% in 2008 and 65.2% in 1983. The Church of England has seen the greatest decline in its numbers; membership has more than halved from 40.3% of the population in 1983 to just 16.3% in 2014.

A 2014 YouGov poll found that 77% of the population did not consider themselves to be religious, including the 40% who said they were not religious at all.

Religiosity is particularly on the wane amongst young people. A 2013

YouGov poll found that only 25% of 16–24-year-olds believe in God, whilst 38% do not believe in either God or a greater spiritual power. The same study found that only 12% of young people pronounced themselves as being influenced by religious leaders.

An Ipsos MORI poll, published in January 2007 for the British Humanist Association, indicated that 36% of people – equivalent to around 17 million adults – are in fact humanist in their basic outlook.

Another question found that 41% endorsed the strong statement: 'This life is the only life we have and death is the end of our personal existence.' 62% chose 'Human nature by itself gives us an understanding of what is right and wrong', against 27% who said 'People need religious teachings in order to understand what is right and wrong'.

In the 2007–08 Citizenship Survey, participants were requested to select factors that they regarded as important to their identity from 13 options. Whilst family was top with 97%, followed by interests (87%), religion ranked bottom at 48%. Religion ranked bottom consistently with all age groups up to 65+, where it only moves up to eleventh. Christians ranked religion as thirteenth as a factor important to their identity.

Church attendance in the UK

The 2014 British Social Attitudes Survey found that 58.4% of the population never attend religious services while only 13.1% of people report going to a religious service once a week or more. Of the 16% of people who define as belonging to the Church of England, 51.9% never attend services and in fact only 10.7% of people who identify with the Church of England report attending church at least weekly. More generally, the 2014 BSA Survey discovered that 58.3% of people who were brought up in a religion never attend services, and only 12.8% do so on a weekly basis.

However, self-reported Church attendance is invariably higher than actual recorded attendance.

According to Religious Trends No 7 published by Christian Research, overall church attendance in the United Kingdom diminished rapidly from 1980 to 2005 in both proportional and real terms.

In 1980, 5,201,300 people, representing 11.1% of the UK population, attended Church on a given Sunday, but by 2005 this number had reduced to 3,166,200, equating to 6.3% of the UK population. By 2015, the level of church attendance in the UK is predicted to fall to 3,081,500 people, or 5% of the population.

The Church of England's own attendance figures also attest to decline; in 2012, average Sunday attendance figures were just 800,000, half the number that attended in 1968 and significantly lower than the 2002 figure of 1,005,000.

Attitudes in the UK

Attitudes towards belief

In a 2007 survey conducted by YouGov on behalf of the broadcaster and writer John Humphries, 42% of the participants believed religion had a harmful effect.

'C of E not important say most people'
YouGov, 2005

In a large-scale YouGov poll of over 3,500 people, the Church of England came 32nd out of 37 in a list of what people think defines Britishness. Only 17% of respondents thought that the Church of England was 'very important' in contributing to a sense of Britishness, while 23% thought it was 'not important at all'.

Families at prayer? As congregations shrink, half of children with two religious parents reject church – ESRC, August 2005

Religious belief is declining faster than attendance at services in the UK, according to a study funded by the ESRC which found that parents' beliefs, practices and affiliations have the biggest impact on children.

65% of young people are not religious. Though religious belief amongst the young has declined by 10% in less than ten years, moral attitudes have not and fewer young people are racially prejudiced.

On 'faith' schools

In June 2014, an Opinium poll found that:

⇨ 58% of the British public was opposed to the existence of state-funded 'faith' schools, with just 30% accepting state funding.

⇨ 70% of those opposed to state funding said this because they think the taxpayer should not be funding religion, 60% because they think 'faith' schools promote division and segregation, and 41% because they think they are contrary to the promotion of a multicultural society.

⇨ 56% of respondents said that faith schools should teach the national curriculum, with only a small minority arguing that they should have significant flexibility over what they teach.

In a ComRes/Accord poll from November 2012, 73% of respondents agreed (and 50% strongly agreed) that 'state-funded schools, including state-funded faith schools, should not be allowed to select or discriminate against prospective pupils on religious grounds in their admissions policy'. Just 18% disagreed.

In an Ipsos MORI poll commissioned by the teachers' union NASUWT and Unison in April 2010, when asked which group is the most appropriate to run state-funded schools, only 4% answered 'religious organisations'. When asked which groups should not run state-funded schools, 35% said religious organisations (the highest figure obtained by any of the answers listed).

In a YouGov/Accord poll from June 2009:

⇨ 57% believed that state-funded schools that selected students according to their religion harm community cohesion.

⇨ 72% agreed or strongly agreed that all schools should implement recruitment and employment policies that do not discriminate on grounds of religion or belief.

⇨ 74% held the view that all state schools should teach an objective and balanced syllabus for education about a wide range of religious and non-religious beliefs.

On assisted dying

Polls taken on the issue of assisted dying consistently demonstrate the majority of the public wish the law to be reformed, and to create a humane and ethical law on assisted dying. A September 2012 YouGov poll commissioned by the BHA found that 81% of UK adults (including 82% of Anglicans and 66% of Catholics) support the notion of mentally competent individuals with incurable or terminal diseases who wish to end their lives receiving medical assistance to do so, without those assisting them facing prosecution.

In May 2014, 73% of respondents to a YouGov/Dignity in Dying poll supported Lord Falconer's proposals to legalise assisted dying for the terminally ill. Only 13% were against the proposals.

Majorities of religious believers support assisted dying. Separate YouGov polls in 2013 found that:

⇨ 78% who attend a place of worship at least monthly support the practice

⇨ 62% of strongly religious people support assisted dying for the terminally ill.

According to the 26th report of the *British Social Attitudes Survey* published in 2010, 71% of religious and 92% non-religious people (82% in total) believe that a doctor should be allowed to end the life of a patient with an incurable disease. The 2012 survey similarly found that 84% of people support assisted dying for the incurably ill.

On abortion and contraception

The *British Social Attitudes Survey* 2012 found that there is an overwhelming consensus in the UK that abortion is justified in cases of:

⇨ a health risk to the parent, with 95% in favour

⇨ the diagnosis of a defect, with 85% in favour

⇨ the parents not wishing to have a child, with 76% in favour.

Only 6% of Catholics questioned in a poll by YouGov for ITV agreed that abortion should never be allowed, and only 11% believed abortion should only be permitted as an indirect consequence of a life-saving treatment for the mother. In contrast, 30% agreed that abortion should be a matter of individual choice, and 44% agreed that abortion should be permitted on grounds of 'rape, incest, severe disability to the child or as an indirect consequence of life-saving treatment for the mother'.

Only 4% of Catholic adults questioned believed artificial contraception is wrong and should not be used. 71% agreed it should be used more often, 23% believed it was a matter entirely for couples.

A 2013 YouGov poll found that the percentage of the population wanting an outright ban on abortion had declined from 12% in 2005, to 7% in 2013. Whilst 44% of those polled agreed that life begins at conception, most of this group did not support a ban on abortion.

The level of support for abortion has been tracked by a series of polls since the 1980s. In the earliest polls 'abortions should be made legally available for all who want it', and this number has generally been slowly rising.

In 2007, the organisation Catholics for Choice commissioned a poll from YouGov on religious opinion towards abortion, and the involvement of Catholic Bishops in the political debate concerning abortion law. In response to the statement: 'It should be legal for a

woman to have an abortion when she has an unwanted pregnancy', 63% of all respondents to the poll strongly agreed or agreed (14% disagreed or strongly disagreed); 58% of self-identified Protestants strongly agreed or agreed (19% disagreed or strongly disagreed); and 43% of self-identified Catholics strongly agreed or agreed (27% disagreed or strongly disagreed).

In response to the statement: 'Catholic bishops concentrate too much of their attention on abortion when there are other issues that also require their attention', 64% of all respondents to the poll strongly agreed or agreed (8% disagreed or strongly disagreed); 68% of self-identified Protestants strongly agreed or agreed (7% disagreed or strongly disagreed); and 42% of self-identified Catholics strongly agreed or agreed (27% disagreed or strongly disagreed).

On medical research

In the *British Social Attitudes Survey*, when asked 'medical research on embryos should probably or definitely be allowed', 61% of religious respondents agreed, compared to 77% non-religious respondents.

On religion and government

A 2012 YouGov poll found that 67% of people do not think that religion should play any role in public life. In general, 51% of people think that religion is declining in Britain.

In the *British Social Attitudes Survey* (2010):

⇨ 75% of those questioned believed their religious leaders should not influence their voting behaviour.

⇨ 67% believe religious leaders should stay out of government decision making.

⇨ 45% of Britons believe that the involvement of religious leaders would have a deleterious effect on policy.

⇨ Only 25% of people believe religious involvement would produce better policy.

⇨ 73% of respondents believe that 'people with very strong

religious beliefs are often too intolerant of others'. This view was held by 82% of people who class themselves as non-religious, and 63% of those who consider themselves religious

The 28th report of the *British Social Attitudes Survey* (2011) also concluded that we can expect to see 'a continued increase in liberal attitudes towards a range of issues such as abortion, homosexuality, same-sex marriage, and euthanasia, as the influence of considerations grounded in religion declines'.

The same report goes on to recommend that: 'The recently expressed sentiment of the current coalition government to 'do' and 'get' God therefore may not sit well with, and could alienate, certain sections of the population.'

On bishops in the House of Lords

A 2012 YouGov poll found that 58% of Britons do not believe that bishops should sit in the House of Lords. 65% of people think that Bishops are out of touch with public opinion.

A 2011 survey for Unlock Democracy found that if the House of Lords was reformed in such a way as to guarantee a residual power of appointment for a limited number of places, only 10.6% of people would think that Bishops would be an appropriate choice.

74% of the British public believe it is wrong that Bishops have an automatic right to a seat in the House of Lords, including 70% of Christians according to an ICM survey conducted in 2010 on behalf of the Joseph Rowntree Reform Trust.

⇨ The above information is reprinted with kind permission from the British Humanist Association. Please visit humanism.org.uk for further information.

© British Humanist Association 2015

The spirit of things unseen: belief in post-religious Britain

For all that formalised religious belief and institutionalised religious belonging has declined over recent decades, the British have not become a nation of atheists or materialists. On the contrary, a spiritual current runs as, if not more, powerfully through the nation than it once did.

⇨ Over three-quarters of all adults (77%) and three-fifths (61%) of non-religious people believe that 'there are things in life that we simply cannot explain through science or any other means.'

⇨ A majority of people (59%) are believers in the existence of some kind of spiritual being, 30% believe in God 'as a universal life force', 30% in spirits, 25% in angels, and 12% in 'a higher spiritual being that can't be called God.'

   • This figure is lower among the non-religious but is still 34%, meaning that over a third of the non-religious believe in the existence of some kind of spiritual being.

⇨ Nearly two in five people believe in the existence of a soul (39%), 32% in life after death, 26% in heaven, 16% in reincarnation, 13% in hell, and 13% in the power of deceased ancestors. In total, over half the British public (54%) holds at least one of these spiritual beliefs.

⇨ By comparison, only 13% of adults – and only 25% of the non-religious – agree with the statement 'humans are purely material beings with no spiritual element'.

⇨ More than half of people – 52% – think spiritual forces have some influence either on Earth, in influencing people's thoughts, events in the human world, or events in the natural world.

   • While 62% of people who call themselves Christians think that spiritual forces have some influence on either people's thoughts, events in the human world, or events in the natural world, over a third (35%) of non-religious people also do.

⇨ A sixth (17%) of people said that prayer works 'in the sense

that it can bring about change for the people or situation you are praying for', a view most likely to be found among elderly respondents (23% of those aged 65+) and religious minorities.

- 36% of people who say they belong to no religion claim that prayer does not work, compared to 6% of people who identified themselves with a religious group.

- The most popular view on prayer, held by 51% of people, is that 'prayer works, in the sense that it makes you feel more at peace'.

⇨ Two in five people (38%) think prayer could heal people, compared with 50% who think it cannot.

- 53% of religious people think prayer could heal people, compared with only 12% of the non-religious.

⇨ A sixth (17%) of people think that 'miracles are the result of God or a higher power intervening in nature', whereas nearly a third (30%) take the opposite view, namely that 'miracles don't exist – they are simply examples of coincidence or luck'.

- The most popular view is, as with prayer, the middle way, in which 42% of people said that 'miracles are unusual events that we cannot yet explain through science'.

⇨ Remarkably, a sixth, or 16%, of people say that they or someone they knew had 'experienced what [they] would call a miracle', with younger respondents being consistently more likely to say this than older ones.

- Even 8% of the non-religious claim that they, or someone they knew, had experienced a miracle.

⇨ Nearly a quarter (23%) of people say they have had their tarot cards read, whilst 17%

have had their star sign read, and 12% have had a reflexology session.

- Smaller numbers had experienced more esoteric spiritual experiences, such as having a reiki session (8%), having their aura read (6%), or healing with crystals (5%).

- Women are considerably more likely than men to undergo these experiences (51% vs 26%).

- Interestingly, while 39% of the overall population admits to having undergone at least one of these experiences, so do 38% of the nonreligious (compared to 40% of the religious). When it comes to these more obviously non-religious spiritual activities, there appears to be no difference according to whether someone is religious or not.

⇨ 11% of people said they had 'visited a spiritual or faith healer, or a religious leader who specialises in praying for the sick'.

- There was no notable difference in the figure across sub-groups for this issue, except among the non-religious, where the figure is 4%.

⇨ 13% of people say they prayed 'daily or more often', 8% say they prayed a few times a week and 34% said they prayed occasionally. Nearly a half, or 45%, of people say they never prayed.

- The majority (81%) of the non-religious say they never prayed, and only 3% said they prayed a few times a week or more often.

⇨ Overall, spiritual beliefs are not the preserve of the elderly, who

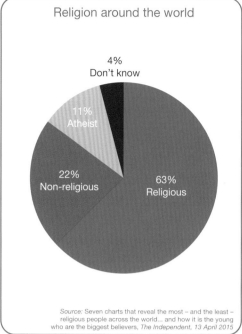

Religion around the world

4% Don't know

11% Atheist

22% Non-religious

63% Religious

Source: Seven charts that reveal the most – and the least – religious people across the world... and how it is the young who are the biggest believers, *The Independent, 13 April 2015*

might be more inclined towards them on account of having grown up in a more religious culture. Such beliefs are to be found across the age ranges.

⇨ Moreover, spiritual beliefs are clearly not the preserve of the 'religious' but are to be found across religious and non-religious groups, although those who consider themselves to belong to a religious group are more likely to hold such beliefs and practices.

ComRes interviewed 2,036 adults from Great Britain online between 4th and 5th September 2013. Data were weighted to be representative of all adults aged 18+ in Great Britain. ComRes is a member of the British Polling Council and abides by its rules.

Published in 2013

⇨ The above information is reprinted with kind permission from Theos. Please visit www.theosthinktank.co.uk for further information.

Britain IS a Christian country (but we're not religious)

While a minority of British people are religious, most people think Britain is a Christian country.

David Cameron risks fostering 'alienation' with his characterisation of Britain as a Christian country, according to an open letter in the *Daily Telegraph* signed by 50 public figures. Responding to comments by the PM that Britain should be 'more evangelical' and 'confident in its status as a Christian country', the letter argued that the British people neither identify with Christianity nor hold Christian beliefs, and therefore it is wrong to 'exceptionalise' Christianity.

New research from YouGov confirms the nuanced attitude that British people take to this issue.

On the one hand, only a minority, 37%, of British people 'regard [themselves] as belonging to' a Christian religion. Half (50%) of the population, including around six in ten under-40s, don't feel they belong to any religion at all.

Plus, the vast majority (77%) of British adults do not describe themselves as religious. That includes four in ten (40%) who say they are 'not religious at all' and another 37% who say they are 'not very religious'. Even among over 60s, the group most likely to identify as religious, only 31% do so, including only a negligible 2% who say they are 'very religious'.

The data support the letter's claim that Britain is – today at least – a 'largely non-religious society'.

Yet this is only half the picture. At the same time, 55% of the public agree with Mr Cameron's claim – that 'Britain is a Christian country'. A third (33%) disagree. 58% also believe that Britain should be a Christian country.

Both questions were also asked two years ago, and views have not changed significantly.

As for the Prime Minister's call for Britain to be more confident in its Christian identity? People tend to agree with that too. YouGov presented respondents with the following excerpt of Mr Cameron's original editorial in *The Church Times* (but made no mention of the PM himself):

I believe we should be more confident about our status as a Christian country, more ambitious about expanding the role of faith-based organisations, and, frankly, more evangelical about a faith that compels us to get out there and make a difference to people's lives.

The British public agree with the statement – by 50% to 35%.

23 April 2014

⇨ The above information is reprinted with kind permission from YouGov. Please visit yougov.co.uk for further information.

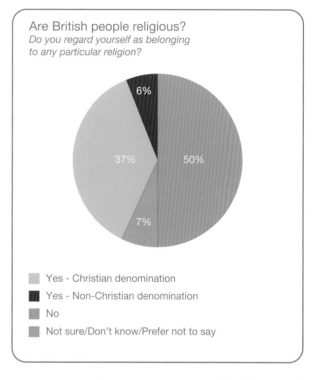

Are British people religious?
Do you regard yourself as belonging to any particular religion?

- 6%
- 50%
- 37%
- 7%

- Yes - Christian denomination
- Yes - Non-Christian denomination
- No
- Not sure/Don't know/Prefer not to say

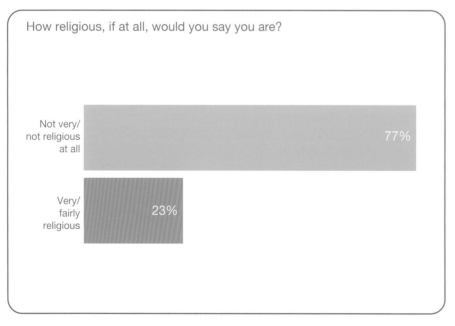

How religious, if at all, would you say you are?

- Not very/not religious at all: 77%
- Very/fairly religious: 23%

Two thirds of people worldwide are religious (but less than one third of Brits)

By Ruth Gledhill

Two thirds of people worldwide are religious, according to a poll of belief in 65 countries. This contrasts with the picture in the UK where two thirds of people are either convinced atheists or not religious, according to Gallup International poll. The poll also shows that worldwide, young people are more religious than older generations, indicating the level of religious belief globally is likely to rise.

In the UK, just three in ten people said they were religious. More than half, 53 per cent, said they were not religious. More than one in ten, 13 per cent, said they were convinced atheists.

In the US, nearly six in ten people, 56 per cent, said they were religious. One third said they were not religious and just six per cent were convinced atheists.

Gallup International researched the religious beliefs of 63,898 people from 65 countries across the globe. They were not asked what their faith was, just whether they were a religious person, not a religious person, a convinced atheist or whether they did not know.

Worldwide, six out of ten, 63 per cent, said they were religious, while one in five, 22 per cent, said they were not and one in ten, 11 per cent, considered themselves convinced atheists. In Africa and the Middle East more than eight out of ten people, 86 per cent and 82 per cent, respectively, portrayed themselves as religious.

China emerged the least religious country with six in ten people stating they were convinced atheists, twice the number of any other country. China is followed by Hong Kong and then Japan, both with more than three in ten espousing atheism.

In the Czech Republic, three in ten said they were atheists and next was the once-devoutly Catholic nation of Spain where one in five people said they were atheists and a further third said they were not religious. Fewer than four in ten people in Spain said they were religious.

The poll showed Thailand to be the most religious country globally with more than nine in ten people being religious. More than nine in ten people said they were religious also in Armenia, Bangladesh, Georgia and Morocco.

Western Europe and Oceania were where opinions were most polarised. In Western Europe, 43 per cent said they were religious and 37 per cent said they were not. It was also in these two regions and in Asia where the largest number of atheists were found – 14 per cent in Western Europe and Asia and 12 per cent in Oceania.

The most religious regions were Africa, the Middle East and North Africa where more than eight in ten considered themselves religious.

In Israel, 65 per cent of those asked said that they were either not religious or convinced atheists, compared to just 30 per cent who said they were religious. In the Palestinian Territories, the West Bank and Gaza, 75 per cent said they were religious compared to 18 per cent who said they were not.

Globally, younger people aged under 34 were more religious – about 66 per cent as against about 60 per cent for the other age groups. The poll found that income was a better indicator of religiosity than education. Among those with a medium high and high income, under half were religious, against seven in ten of those with low, medium low and medium incomes. Likewise, the number of convinced atheists was as high as 22 per cent and 25 per cent among people with medium-high and high income but only six per cent and five per cent among people with low and medium low income.

Jean-Marc Leger, president of WIN/Gallup International Association, said:

'Religion continues to dominate our everyday lives and we see that the total number of people who consider themselves to be religious is actually relatively high. Furthermore, with the trend of an increasingly religious youth globally, we can assume that the number of people who consider themselves religious will only continue to increase.'

13 April 2015

⇨ The above information is reprinted with kind permission from Christian Today. Please visit www.christiantoday.com for further information.

Should the UK adopt the French approach to religion and become a secularist state?

Yes because:

The UK should adopt a secular model as practised by the French and Germans where there is a complete separation of the state and religion; with protection and equal treatment afforded to all faiths without preference to any one faith. The Church of England should finally be disestablished with the Queen no longer being the Supreme Head of the Church. Finally, the last remaining bishops should be removed from the House of Lords and from the legislative process of the country.

No because:

No, because the French secular model has ultimately undermined religion and the right to freedom of religion to the extent that any form of religious identity in public is criticised, illegal or shunned. Instead of a religious person being able to become a leading politician or judge, secular ones are promoted. Secular has come to mean atheistic. Religious figures have succeeded in Britain, no matter their religious affiliation. Britain's system has ultimately created real freedom, while France tries to create a religious free society. Not all religion can be kept to the confines of a house, such as the issue over the hijab.

A secular Britain would not provide greater religious equality for the 'minority' faiths at the expense of Christianity, but would damage all faiths. Ultimately, if it isn't broken, then don't try to fix it. If we were to become a secular state the monarchy would have to be replaced, as well as the introduction of a great deal of change, which goes against British historical development.

The slowing decline of religion – and the generational challenge for Christianity

The proportion of the total population who see themselves as belonging to a particular religion has been on the decline – from around two-thirds (65%) back in the mid-1980s to just over half (53%) by 2011. That's not particularly surprising or new – the Census figures released last year show a similar decline, although differences in the question mean the proportions are different.[1]

This is quite a fall – the sort of change that would raise concern for the long-term survival of religious attachment. This decline, however, is almost entirely related to changes in the generational make-up of the population, similar to the patterns we've seen with political attachment.

As with political identification, there is very flat affiliation with a religion within each generation over time – and each has a lower level of religious attachment than their elders. But having said that, the gaps between generations are getting successively smaller, so that there is little difference between generation X and generation Y, and in fact it is the pre-war generation that stand out as particularly different.

Of course, generational effects are far from all that's going on in religious trends. As the Census highlights, it's actually Christianity that's declining, while all the other main religions are increasing (mostly related to immigration). But given these make up a very small proportion of the overall religious community, the aggregate trend has still been firmly downwards.

However, there has actually been no change in attendance at religious services or meetings over this period. One in five people (21%) claimed to attend religious services once a month or more in 1989, and exactly the same percentage (21%) claimed to do so in 2011 – and there was remarkable consistency throughout the intervening years. These contrasting trends of decreasing affiliation and stable regular religious attendance are in line with other studies that show that much of the decline is among cultural or nominal Anglicans, while the number with an active faith remains steady.

And this is partly down to the shifting generational patterns of attendance. Up until the mid-2000s there was a very similar generational pattern to that seen with affiliation, with each successive generation less likely to attend than the previous. But this has changed significantly, if somewhat erratically, for the two youngest generations – so that by 2011, these generations were actually more likely to say they regularly attend services than baby boomers.

As Grace Davie outlines, this all seems to support the view that the church is moving from a conscript to a professional army.[2] And this seems to be playing out generationally, as a simple comparison of the ratio of affiliation to attendance suggests; there are much lower 'conversion rates' from affiliation to attendance among the pre-war generation than there are among younger generations.

Of course this raises the question of why we're seeing this shifting pattern – and in particular whether it is driven by the higher proportions of younger people with attachment to non-Christian religions (for example, as a result of the age profile of recent immigrants).

Unfortunately, this is difficult to answer definitively with the data here, as the sample sizes are too small to break down by religion within generation. However, it seems likely to be at least part of

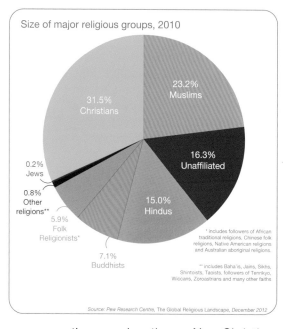

Size of major religious groups, 2010

- 31.5% Christians
- 23.2% Muslims
- 16.3% Unaffiliated
- 15.0% Hindus
- 7.1% Buddhists
- 5.9% Folk Religionists*
- 0.8% Other religions**
- 0.2% Jews

* includes followers of African traditional religions, Chinese folk religions, Native American religions and Australian aboriginal religions.

** includes Baha'is, Jains, Sikhs, Shintoists, Taoists, followers of Tenrikyo, Wiccans, Zoroastrians and many other faiths

Source: Pew Research Centre, The Global Religious Landscape, December 2012

the explanation. Non-Christians make up a significantly greater proportion of the religious within this youngest age group. This means that the gap between generation Y and generation X is greater on Christianity than overall religious attachment.

So the overall picture of religious attachment and attendance looks perhaps more stable in the long run than many would expect: it seems inevitable that we will see further declines in belonging, but at a slowing rate – and attendance figures may actually continue to hold up remarkably well.

However, unfortunately for Christian churches, this is not incompatible with Lord Carey's suggestion today that Christianity is just 'a generation away from extinction' without concerted action to bring young people back in.

⇨ The above information is reprinted with kind permission from Ipsos MORI. Please visit www.ipsos-mori-generations. com for further information.

1 For example, Lee, L. (2011) British Social Attitudes 28, Chapter 12.

2 Grace Davie, *What are the main Trends in Religion and Values in Britain?*

Can the Church of England attract young people again?

Andrew Grey argues the Church of England should ignore gimmicks and attract the youth with its authentic message.

The Church of England needs more young people. This drum has been banged on repeat for years: 'it needs to be more relevant'; 'young people are put off the church' – the Archbishop of York even issued a prophetic-sounding warning in 2013 that the church is 'one generation away from extinction'.

Enter Rob Popejoy: Chaplain at the City of Bath College. He's something of a hipster: he sports a beard at the age of 30, wears beanie hats and owns a skateboard. He is also heavily tattooed, and has interests in snowboarding, football and hip-hop.

Surely this man is the answer to all our prayers? When young people see the church as stuffy and outdated, this man can bring a breath of fresh air. He embraces his students' interests with vigour, even getting involved in one student's project by being photographed topless, covered in paint and wearing just a bow tie.

SOMEHOW IT JUST FEELS LIKE THE REAL THING!

Oh, and he's covered in tattoos.

But whilst Popejoy may seem original, he is in fact following an ongoing tradition of gimmicky ways to attract young people. For at least the past two decades, a growing number of churches have gone out of their way to try to convince young people that they are cool enough for us: they don't need boring old organs when they've got electric guitars, or dusty old hymnbooks, when they've got a laptop and projector. All young people need to do is give them a try.

The problem with all of these gestures, well-intentioned as they are, is that they are superficial. Countless churches have made these transformations, and sure, maybe they attract one or two more young people than they would otherwise – but our cries of a dying church have not gone away.

These gestures are largely unsuccessful because they are often inauthentic. As a 25-year-old – surely one of the Church of England's target audience – I've felt extremely uncomfortable listening to middle-aged men wearing jeans demanding I lift my hands in worship as they strum their guitars. I feel much more comfortable in my current local church – a twelfth-century building with an organ and pews. This isn't just because I happen to have grown fond of that style – it's also, and perhaps more, about the fact that it's genuine. Neither the vicar nor the congregation pretend to be something that they're not.

This isn't to say that churches shouldn't

use guitars or screens. If that's genuinely what makes the congregation comfortable, and facilitates worship most effectively, then of course a church should use this. Similarly, if a Chaplain like Rob Popejoy genuinely feels comfortable on a skateboard and wants to use it, why not? These things aren't inherently inauthentic. But they should never be done for the purpose of simply trying to appeal to young people – because we can see through it.

Authenticity matters to people of my generation. Obviously, it isn't just the young who appreciate it. But it has particular meaning to us. Why? Because, in truth, it's the one thing that is a universal struggle for people of younger generations to obtain. Teenagers go out of their way to style their hair; many schoolgirls start to experiment with make-up as they learn, very quickly, that their natural face just isn't good enough for the real world.

University students leave home and struggle to find out who they are. They try new clubs and societies, and spend a lot of time getting as drunk as possible, and/or remodelling their fashion, music taste, film taste – anything to help them develop a persona that will make people like them.

Then they leave university and find that they have to turn themselves into the ideal worker, despite having little or no experience of the working world. They have to go to job interviews and convince strangers that they're the ideal independent worker and team-player; that their decisions are both made quickly and well thought out; that they are easy to get along with but take their work very seriously; that they will put in the hours but strike the perfect – cliché alert – 'work-life balance'.

Frankly, it's no wonder young people struggle for authenticity. We spend so much time trying to be accepted by every different person and group imaginable that we never have space to work out just who we are.

And this is where the church really should come in. Rather than trying its best to mimic young people's transient fashions and trends, it should be offering the message that young people – indeed all people – desperately need to hear: you are accepted. More than accepted – you are loved. Your worth isn't dependent on your academic achievements, or your job title or salary; it's not about how cool or attractive you are; and it doesn't matter how interesting your hobbies sound. Your worth comes from the fact that you are a human being – it is innate, and cannot be taken away. You were fearfully and wonderfully made.

Of course, one problem with this, as is often lamented, is the difficulty of telling young people that they're accepted when there appear to be limits. It's no good telling a young woman that she's accepted by God but could never be a leader in the church because of her gender. Or telling her that she's very welcome to come into the church, but her friends who are in a same-sex relationships must stay away. That's not acceptance.

If the church is to be truly 'relevant', it should stop treating young people as naïve airheads who will gravitate towards anything that looks vaguely 'young', and realise that what it can offer us is the gospel message – in word and deed – of God's unconditional love and acceptance.

16 February 2015

⇨ The above information is reprinted with kind permission from On Religion. Please visit www.onreligion.co.uk for further information.

Soldiers still turn to the Bible today

By Hazel Southam

Soldiers who turned to the Bible and prayer whilst on the front line in Afghanistan have described their experiences in a new study published in the 2013 *Defence Academy Yearbook*.

British troops serving today told how they carried Bibles, crucifixes and rosaries whilst deployed abroad.

The survey was carried out by the Reverend Peter King, an army chaplain. He was based in Helmand Province in Afghanistan between October 2011 and April 2012.

He said, 'The significance of scripture and prayer is still there for soldiers. It surprised me how the Bible is still valued in a very different society from World War One.

'If you are faced with the possibility of danger, it seems to be when the ultimate questions are asked.

'People will carry Bibles passed down through the family. That's about a link with loved ones.

'But there's also evidence that scripture became a rock, a source of guidance, or a place where hope was found. One soldier said he read his Bible because "it gave me belief that if I made the ultimate sacrifice I had something to go to".

Of those responding in the survey, some 46% said that they prayed while they were in Afghanistan and a further 46% carried a symbol of faith, often including a Bible. One soldier had written Bible references on his protective kneepads.

King's survey revealed that 42.5% said that they were more likely to pray while in proximity to danger, and 63% said that they were more likely to attend religious services on Operations than when in Barracks.

75 per cent described themselves as Christian, 12% as atheist, 7% as agnostic and the remainder followed another faith, belief or philosophy.

Those joining the Armed Forces today are still offered a copy of the Bible, just as they were in 1914.

'The attitude towards the Bible is positive,' Reverend King said. 'We still have a very significant take-up. And it's used in vigils for repatriation and at Remembrance Sunday when it speaks a language that's understood by soldiers.'

Mr King said that while everyone is ultimately faced with the profound questions of life, soldiers face them at a young age because 'they face dangers more than most people'. The Bible, he said, helped some of them find answers to those questions.

Last updated 22 October 2014

⇨ The above information is reprinted with kind permission from the Bible Society. Please visit www.biblesociety.org.uk for further information.

Muslims in Europe: questions and answers

As anti-Muslim manifestations increase in Europe, particularly in the aftermath of the Paris and Copenhagen attacks, we clarify some misconceptions and answer some of the most frequent questions about Muslims in Europe.

Q: Who are Muslim Europeans?

Muslims have been present in Europe since the 7th century. Diplomacy and trade exchanges have always existed between the Muslim world and Europe. After World War II, a large immigrant labour force coming primarily from Mediterranean countries with majority Muslim populations were recruited to support rebuilding efforts in Europe. Nowadays, Muslim communities are as diverse as European countries are. Different ethnic and cultural origins, nationalities, political views, social classes mean that there is no such thing as one 'Muslim community'. While in Europe, Islam is often associated with Arabs, the latter make up only 15% of the world's Muslim population. Muslims refer to different understandings and lectures of the Islamic literature and to a great variety of theological, juridical and spiritual schools, obedience and traditions. Muslims are spread across the spectrum of potential religious practice: from total non-practice to intensive practice – the level of practice evolving also during a lifetime. Levels of practice differ also according to the religious practice: whereas estimates consider that only 10% of Muslims are engaging in regular prayers, more than 70% tend to respect fasting during the month of Ramadan.

Q: How many Muslims are there in Europe?

Most EU countries do not collect data disaggregated by religion in censuses, so it is impossible to know exactly how many Muslims live in Europe. However, research based on proxies has estimated that around 19 million Muslims live in Europe, which represents 6% of the total European population. Populist and far-right parties tend to increase this number to support the argument of an 'Islamisation of Europe'. Recent public opinion surveys have shown that the number of European Muslims is often overestimated. A 2014 survey found that French respondents thought that 31% of their compatriots were Muslim, while actual figures show that only 8% of French residents are Muslims – including non-practising Muslims. UK respondents thought there were 21% Muslims in Britain, when they constitute only 5% of the British population.

Q: Are all Muslims violent, terrorist extremists?

While there is no single interpretation of Islam, renowned Islamic authorities across the world have repeatedly affirmed that terrorism cannot be justified by the teachings of their religion, which aims to promote justice and peace. Muslim leaders and scholars often speak out against terrorism and seek to counter misinterpreted or twisted teachings based on a theology of violence and death that fringe groups use to justify their violent actions. Most Muslims feel as threatened as anyone else by these violent extremists who say they act in the name of Islam. Muslims have been the target of terrorist attacks too, and are in no way protected because of their religion. To date, worldwide, Muslims suffer the highest death toll due to jihadist terror groups. Some of the victims of the Paris attacks were Muslims.

Q: If all Muslims are not terrorists, are all terrorists Muslims?

A survey conducted by the Centre for Research on Globalization found that the terrorists acts perpetrated by Muslim extremists constitute only 2.5% of all terrorist attacks on US soil between 1970 and 2012. In 2013, 152 terrorist attacks occurred in Europe with only one attack being religiously motivated while 84 were motivated by ethno-nationalist or separatist beliefs. The massive media coverage of Muslim extremists' acts contributes to feeding the myth that all terrorist acts are perpetrated by Muslims. Far-right movements are also a form of extremism present in Europe, which poses a similar threat to society and peaceful coexistence.

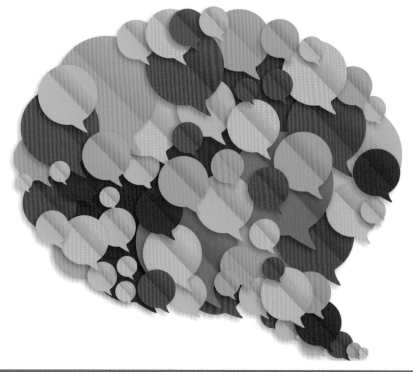

Q: Do Muslims agree with the Paris and Copenhagen terror attacks?

Some Muslims have felt offended by some of Charlie Hebdo's cartoons. But this in no way means that they support the deadly attacks. Most Muslim organisations publically condemned these murders, recalling that words should be countered with words, and that Islam shouldn't be used as a way to justify terror attacks. Many of these organisations were present on 11 January to peacefully march in Paris and other French and European capitals. A number of European Muslim intellectuals have also insisted on the importance of freedom of expression.

Q: Are European Muslims increasingly anti-Semites?

Anti-Semitism is not new in Europe and is still very much present across European society. Muslims are not immune to anti-Semitism. Some Muslims are influenced by theological discourses rooted in anti-Semitism, far-right ideologues, negationists and those spreading confusion between Israel and Jews in general. However, a recent Pew Research Centre study shows that negative opinions on Jews are growing in Europe, reaching 25% of unfavourable opinion in Germany, where only 6% of the population is Muslim. In Spain, where less than 3% of the population is Muslim, close to 50% of the population hold negative opinions about Jews. In France, research and surveys have showed that an 'old' type of far-right anti-Semitism is still dominant and goes hand in hand with other forms of prejudice, including Islamophobia. Affirmations that Muslims are the only source of anti-Semitism in Europe are based on an attempt to pit Jews and Muslims against each other, divide society and spread both Islamophobia and anti-Semitism.

Q: What are the consequences of the Paris attacks on Muslim communities?

Muslims have been publicly called to condemn the attacks, implying that Muslims intrinsically support the perpetrators of the attacks. As a consequence, some Muslims have feared retaliation. The attacks took place in a context of growing Islamophobia in Europe (47% increase in recorded Islamophobic acts in France in 2013 compared to 2012), anti-Muslim marches organised by the far-right Pegida movement, and regular attacks of mosques in Sweden. From 7 January 2015 to 7 February 2015, there were 153 Islamophobic incidents against individuals and places of worship in France, which represents a 70% increase compared to January 2014.

Q: Are young Muslims in Europe becoming more radicalised?

Discrimination and social exclusion are key factors leading young Muslims, among others, to feel excluded and humiliated in Europe and become easy targets for radicalisation. It is necessary to address social segregation and discrimination in employment to include those who no longer believe in the structures that regulate our societies: families, education and employment.

Former and current armed conflicts in the Middle East and beyond have left abandoned populations in chaos in countries that are not able to guarantee a minimum level of security. These conflicts are used in narratives and easily spread by violent extremists to justify terrorist acts. This propaganda is widely spread via social media and mostly appealing to young people's emotions. Worrying trends show an increase of the number of European young Muslims leaving to join jihadist organisations. However, estimates show that these represent less than 0.1% of the total Muslim youth.

Q: What is Islamophobia? How can it be a form of racism as Islam is not a race?

Islamophobia is a specific form of racism that refers to acts of violence and discrimination, as well as racist speech, fuelled by historical abuses and negative stereotyping and leading to exclusion and dehumanisation of Muslims, and all those perceived as such. Islamophobia can also be the result of structural discrimination. Islamophobia is a form of racism in the sense that it is the result of the social construction of a group as a race and to which specificities and stereotypes are attributed. These characteristics are considered genetic (for instance 'Islam is violent, thus Muslims and their kids are violent'). Consequently, even those who choose not to practise Islam but who are perceived as Muslim are subjected to discrimination. Islamophobia has nothing to do with criticism of Islam. Islam, as a religion, as an ideology, is subject to criticism as any other religion or ideology.

Q: Is racial profiling the solution to prevent radicalism?

Data mining and surveillances practices have not yielded conclusive results on combating terrorism or radicalisation. These data collection practices can lead to discriminatory practices and prohibited processing of data revealing race, ethnic origin or religion through the use of proxies. Information such as residency status, home address, nationality, place of birth, phone calls to certain countries, time of bank operations or physical appearance (a beard, a veil, etc.) can be used to racially profile individuals. Racial profiling is a form of racial discrimination that is prohibited under international law. It is also ineffective and counter-productive in that it alienates the very communities whose support is necessary for fighting crime and terrorism. Racial profiling is not effective in terms of law enforcement. Policing depends on cooperation from the public to report crime, provide suspect descriptions and give witness testimonies. Research shows that poor police-citizen contacts and bad treatment by law enforcement officers can have a negative impact on public confidence in law enforcement and also result in reduced cooperation with the latter.

20 February 2015

⇨ The above information is reprinted with kind permission from the European Network Against Racism (ENAR). Please visit www.enar-eu.org for further information.

Ramadan fasting: modern opposition to age-old rules

As Ramadan begins, some Muslims in the West (and north) say ancient customs from the Arabian desert need updating.

By Tehmina Kazi

It's that time of year again. Gentle squabbles over moon sightings, the stockpiling of frozen samosas and the dreaded 'Ramadan breath', which means we have to keep a miswak teeth-cleaning stick (or, more likely, a toothbrush) on us at all times. For tomorrow is the start of Ramadan, the ninth month of the Islamic calendar.

This kicks off four weeks of introspection (maybe), God-consciousness (hopefully) and abstinence from food, water, smoking and marital sex (you're having a laugh, aren't you?) during daylight hours. The only exemptions from fasting are for older people or those with medical conditions, as well as children (who may fast if they wish to). Further, menstruating women can expect a break during their time of the month.

Faced with the intricacies and possible etiquette blips of these rituals in a country where non-Muslims are in the majority, you'd think advice from a compassionate and highly intelligent scholar would be lapped up. However, over the past few days, my Facebook feed has been heaving with high-handed dismissals of Dr Usama Hasan's excellent juristic opinion, or fatwa, on the reduction of fasting hours. He reasons that summertime fasts in northern Europe are far longer than they were possibly intended to be, with the worshipper receiving only five hours of eating and drinking time in one 24-hour period. After going through the religious precedents in detail, he encourages people who want to keep these long fasts to continue, but states that it is acceptable for others to keep 12- or 16-hour fasts if that is more comfortable for them.

The original principle of the fast (empathy with the poor, charity, service to humanity) is maintained, but it is fused with common sense and an awareness of practical considerations. This goes a step further than the usual dispensations for Muslims whose health is affected, and has ruffled a lot of feathers. Social-media blatherers wrongly accused Dr Hasan of instituting 12-hour fasts for all British Muslims, and tried to make out that he was subordinating God's will to the 'desires' of human beings, failing to see that one of the highest virtues is actually reason.

The issue of fasting becomes even more politicised when children are concerned. Even under orthodox interpretations of Islamic law, as mentioned above, fasting is not obligatory for those who have not entered puberty. This doesn't stop some parents and children going ahead with the practice in school hours, however.

One primary-school trust grew so concerned about children fainting, becoming ill or missing out on parts of the curriculum, that it banned fasting this month. Justin James, the chief executive of the Lion Academy Trust, which covers a number of schools in east London, cited the delicate balancing act of the school's obligations under child-protection law versus working with the local communities it serves. It is a balance that my organisation, British Muslims for Secular Democracy, knows only too well. We recently received funding to revise and update our advice for schools, which helps teachers to negotiate these thorny issues, establish open channels of communication with parents and find the best outcome for everyone concerned.

In many Muslim communities, there is a knee-jerk negative reaction to anything progressive or sensible, with certain people assuming that these measures automatically 'water down' the faith. This is borne of an insecurity which deems the most severe version of a religion to be the most 'authentic', and means that dissenting voices end up feeling isolated and unheard. A friend was recently looking to interview some non-fasting Muslims in Yorkshire. Hardly anyone answered her call, and her original request was met with snorts of derision on Facebook.

Contrary to what the snorters may think, their actions represent a departure from the spirit of this month, where people are supposed to work on their own spirituality and actions. Some of my best Ramadan memories involve dishing out fried chicken to homeless people at Lincoln's Inn (with Muslims and non-Muslims), and having the accompanying dhal and bananas handed right back with a cheeky grin. It would be great to see more of these events emblazoned on to the public consciousness, rather than toy-throwing defensiveness and exceptionalism.

Tehmina Kazi is the director of British Muslims for Secular Democracy.

16 June 2015

⇨ The above information is reprinted with kind permission from *The Independent*. Please visit www.independent.co.uk for further information.

Of little faith: world's most dangerous places for atheists

As an Afghan citizen who is an atheist secures UK asylum for religious reasons, Channel 4 News looks at some of the countries where it is illegal to have no faith.

Afghanistan

In Afghanistan the constitution and other laws often contradict themselves on freedom of religion or belief, and freedom of expression.

But overall, these rights are severely restricted and frequently violated by the government, as well as by regional and local chiefs, and non-state actors.

For example, despite constitutional guarantees of freedom of religion, apostasy is still punishable by death.

Iran

The Iranian constitution divides citizens of the Islamic Republic of Iran into four religious categories: Muslims, Zoroastrians, Jews and Christians.

Non-believers are effectively left out and are not afforded any rights or protections.

They must declare their faith in one of the four officially recognised religions in order to be able to claim a number of legal rights, such as the possibility of applying for the general examination to enter any university in Iran.

Malaysia

Every Malaysian citizen over the age of 12 must carry an identification card, a 'MyKad', which must state the bearer's religion.

According to Sharia law within most Malaysian states, apostasy or conversion is a punishable offence, either with a fine, a jail sentence or the death penalty.

Maldives

The constitution designates Islam as the official state religion, and the government and many citizens at all levels interpret this provision as imposing a requirement that all citizens must be Muslims.

Every citizen of the Maldives is required to be a Muslim, and the penalty for leaving Islam is death.

Nigeria

The constitution and other laws and policies protect freedom of thought, conscience and religion, as well as freedom of opinion and expression.

However, these rights are frequently violated by federal, state and local governments, as well as by non-state militias and terrorist groups, such as the violent Islamist group Boko Haram.

Pakistan

The widespread prosecution of cases of alleged blasphemy, which is punishable by death, remains a severe violation of freedom of thought in Pakistan.

The constitution establishes Islam as the state religion.

Qatar

Capital punishment is still on the books for apostasy and blasphemy, and is punishable by up to seven years in prison.

Islam is the state religion and Sharia is the main source of legislation. The law does not recognise religions or belief systems outside the three Abrahamic faiths of Islam, Christianity, and Judaism.

Saudi Arabia

There is no freedom of religion or belief, or freedom of expression, in the kingdom of Saudi Arabia. Punishment for any perceived criticism of the ruling family or ruling form of Islam is swift and severe.

There is no separation between state and religion, and the deep connection between the royal family and the religious establishment results in significant pressure on all citizens to adhere to the official government interpretation of Islam.

Somalia

Somalia has lacked an effective central government for decades. The resulting anarchy has enabled extremist Islamist groups to impose harsh forms of Sharia (Islamic law) that included death for apostasy, blasphemy and other expressions of freedom of belief and expression.

Sudan

The interim national constitution and other laws and policies establish Islam as the source of all legislation, and restrict freedom of religion or belief, freedom of expression, and freedom of assembly and association.

In practice, the government not only enforces these restrictions, but also uses extra-legal violence to violate the rights of it citizens.

United Arab Emirates

The UAE constitution and other laws and policies do not protect freedom or thought, conscience and religion, nor do they protect freedom of opinion and expression.

The constitution declares that Islam is the official religion of all seven constituent emirates of the federal union and defines all citizens as Muslims.

The law also denies Muslims the freedom to change religion or leave Islam.

Others

Four western countries are rated 'severe' because they can jail people for breaking laws prohibiting 'blasphemy' and other free speech on religion.

Those countries are Iceland (a sentence of jail for up to three months), Denmark (up to four months), New Zealand (up to a year), Poland (up to two years), Germany (up to three years) and Greece (up to three years).

Jail time could be handed to someone who simply 'blasphemes God' in the case of Greece, or 'insults the content of other's religious faith' in the case of Germany.

14 January 2014

⇨ An extract from Channel 4 News. Please visit www.channel4.com/news for further information.

Britain's 'atheist church' now pulls in crowds from Berlin to Ohio

Atheism is big business for the founders of Sunday Assembly, who have swapped hymns for pop and sermons for secular lectures.

By Rebecca Burn-Callander, Enterprise Editor

Atheist 'church' the Sunday Assembly has become an international phenomenon, boasting 63 'parishes' across the globe.

The business offers non-believers an alternative to a traditional religious service. Services take place twice a month on a Sunday.

Founded by two former comedians, Sanderson Jones and Pippa Evans, in 2013, the business was launched as a way to 'celebrate life', bring communities together and combat loneliness.

'Pippa left her church very young and missed the community but not the faith,' Mr Jones told *The Telegraph*. 'My mother died when I was very young, which taught me how precious life is. I wanted to find a way to celebrate it in a non-religious way.'

The first event took place in the deconsecrated Union Chapel in London in July last year. Some 300 people attended the launch.

A typical Sunday Assembly consists of a sing-along (pop songs rather than hymns), a secular reading, a talk that helps the congregation 'live better, help often or wonder more' – the company's mantra – followed by a moment of reflection, then tea and cake.

The company has attracted a wide range of speakers, from TV presenters such as Loyd Grossman, Sandi Toksvig and Dan Snow to comedians Arthur Smith and Marcus Brigstocke. It will also be offering a humanist Remembrance Day service on 2 November in London and an alternative Christmas assembly, Yule Rock, also in London, on 18 December.

Sunday Assembly was created as a community organisation. It is free to attend and the assemblies spread virally through volunteers, supported by the founders in London. 'We give them the tools and the branding and website and try to help with marketing,' explained Mr Jones. 'It's not a franchise, but it uses franchising techniques.'

The business is currently for profit, funded through donations from the congregations, but there are plans to reinvent it as a charity with a for-profit company that runs alongside.

The company also closed a £33,000 crowdfunding round last year. A high net worth individual, who prefers to remain anonymous, pledged £25,000 to help grow the network. 'We still have a bit of runway left, but we need help,' said Mr Jones. 'We're actively looking for advice and money right now.'

Financing the Sunday Assembly is fraught with challenges, given its quasi-religious nature. 'No one likes money lenders in the temple,' admitted Mr Jones. 'It's an emotional area.'

To generate revenue, the founders are currently exploring several options: T-shirts and other merchandise may be launched by this Christmas; a Sunday Assembly festival has been mooted, which would charge for tickets; and there is also a membership option for regular 'worshippers'. 'It's a way for our supporters to contribute,' he said.

London remains the biggest parish for Sunday Assembly, with 400 people regularly attending events. Even fast growing hubs such as Amsterdam, Berlin, Paris and Brussels draw fewer than half that.

The Sunday Assembly concept has also taken off in the US.

'We have three in Ohio,' said Mr Jones. 'I'm going to do a talk at our Silicon Valley one on November 9 via robot telepresence. Imagine the headlines,' he said, laughing. 'Robotic preacher addresses atheist church.'

The 'atheist church' mocker has attracted criticism from Christian factions. The Blaze, an American Christian website, received hundreds of comments for its article *Godless congregation: atheist church steals from Christian tradition to launch rapidly-expanding house of worship.*

'You know how little girls play "house"?' wrote one. 'This is grown ups playing "soul".'

'We're super positive about what churches and mosques do,' said Mr Jones. 'We don't bash them and a lot of religious people attend our events.' The issue of loneliness, especially in big cities, is one that must be tackled by religious and non-religious organisations alike, he said.

'People are getting lonelier. We spend so much time connected to social networks that we forget to connect to our friends.'

A recent poll of Sunday Assembly's congregation found that 87% of those who come more than five times are happier, 80% are more satisfied with their life, and feel a part of a community.

These people also had an average of 3.5 more friends as a result of attending Sunday Assembly events. 'This is really important as social isolation is a big problem today,' said Mr Jones.

There are even economic benefits to creating communities like Sunday Assembly, he said. 'The population is ageing, and communities are going to have to look after each other. The state is spending less so we need solutions that help people.'

Some 35 new Sunday Assembly parishes launched this year, and the growth is set to continue. Launching new assemblies is easy, according to Mr Jones, but supporting the existing ones can be more challenging. 'We've worked out how to scale, but making them sustainable is the key.'

Sao Paulo will launch next year,' he added. 'In five years, who knows? Maybe there will be a 1,000 or 10,000. If you'd asked me where we'd be today I never would have guessed we'd be here.'

21 October 2014

⇨ The above information is reprinted with kind permission from *The Telegraph*. Please visit www.telegraph.co.uk for further information.

'House of Religions' bringing eight faiths together under one roof in Bern

There are separate churches, mosques and temples for five faiths.

By Lizzie Dearden

As the Paris attacks and anti-Islam Pegida marches in Germany have spread division and fear among followers of different faiths in Europe, a revolutionary project in Switzerland is uniting eight religions.

The Haus der Religionen (House of Religions) in Bern houses a Christian church, Hindu temple, Buddhist centre, Alevi cemevi and soon, a mosque.

The five private religious spaces open into a shared 'dialogue room' where members of different faiths eat, meet and hold events for the community.

Baha'i, Jewish and Sikh representatives are also part of the Haus, which started as a small group's dream a decade ago and opened in a purpose-built building in December.

While there are other multi-faith centres around the world, the Haus der Religionen is ground-breaking in its scale – five purpose-built homes for five religions. The decorators for the Hindu temple were flown in from India.

If numbers are anything to go by, it is already a resounding success.

An estimated 10,000 people turned up on its opening day and tours are fully booked until the end of April.

Guido Albisetti, president of the foundation behind the Haus, told *The Independent* its founders had been 'overwhelmed' by the support.

'People were queuing outside in the snow for 45 minutes to get in in the freezing weather – we were overflowing,' he added.

The reception was not always so positive. Before the building was constructed in October, vandals broke into the Muslim association planning their new mosque in the Haus, destroyed plans and defaced a picture of the imam.

Mr Albisetti, 62, said the Muslim community in Bern was the only one out of the eight religions to meet internal opposition to involvement with the Haus der Religionen.

'Our imam is very liberal and very strong-minded,' he added. 'More conservative groups had a problem with him.'

But that did not stop the Bern Muslim Association's involvement with the project and their mosque is due to open in March.

The imam, Mustafa Memeti, has just been named Swiss of the Year by the newspaper *SonntagsZeitung* for 'his courage and his engagement in the most explosive debate of our time'.

Also the head of the Albanian Islamic Association of Switzerland, he is known for his vocal support for integration and emphasises that Muslims can be Swiss citizens without losing their identity or religion.

Mr Albisetti, who said he believes in god but does not attend a particular church, said Mr Memeti's stance has become even more vital after the Paris attacks.

'He's trying to find a way that Muslims and all other Swiss religious people live together in a peaceful way.'

In the wake of the massacre at *Charlie Hebdo*, the Haus issued a joint statement simply titled 'je suis Charlie', calling for 'compassion and dialogue' to overpower hatred and fear.

'When Anders Breivik massacred 77 young people to 'save the Christian West' in Norway, no one blamed the whole of Christianity for it, along with their churches and followers in Switzerland,' it said.

'But now, Muslims in our country have to justify themselves after the Paris attacks because some people suspect they are involved.'

But the Haus is fostering acceptance and interaction, hosting visits by schools and groups from all over Switzerland and beyond as well as regular language classes and events.

Bern is a diverse place – more than a third of the city's population are foreign-born, mostly European workers, and although most residents belong to the Swiss Reformed Church, there are thousands of Muslims, Hindus and people of numerous other faiths.

At the opening of the Haus, a Jewish representative read an extract from the Torah before giving the stage to a Muslim who read from the Koran.

Mr Albisetti said the scene was a far cry from what he had seen in Jerusalem, where Christian, Muslim and Jewish holy places are crowded together but deeply divided – 'the example of what we don't want'.

'We're trying to explain to everyone that we accept all religions here as long as it's peaceful,' he added.

'Anyone is welcome in this country as long as they accept everyone else.'

Many of those involved in the Haus have been working together for years, moving from place to place until the dream of having their own premises was made a reality with 15 million Swiss Francs (£10.6 million) of funding.

It is housed in a much larger building containing flats, shops and restaurants in a large square.

'The idea was to put this in the middle of life – not stand it alone like St Peter's in Rome,' Mr Albisetti said. 'The religions have to live in life.'

The 62-year-old still works as a private banker and after years working towards the Haus der Religionen, will be joining its other directors to hand it over to another generation next year.

'We are very fortunate in life. We have good jobs, we have the chance to live in the country where we were born and we just wanted to give something to those people who are not so lucky,' he said.

'It's what we dreamed of – we don't know if it will work for the next 200 years but at the moment everyone works together.'

10 February 2015

⇨ The above information is reprinted with kind permission from *The Independent*. Please visit www.independent.co.uk for further information.

Young people's attitudes to religion

There is strong evidence for a generational effect in declining religious identification among the UK's population. Each successive generation has less attachment to religion but the differences between generations are decreasing. Whereas 72% of those born before 1945 would regard themselves as belonging to a religion, the figure is 51% for Baby Boomers, 40% for Generation X and 38% for Generation Y.[1] 27% of the Pre-War generation regard religion as very important in their lives, twice as many as for all younger generations.[2] It appears that this trend has been driven by a reduction in affiliation with the Church of England, which has halved, whilst affiliation with other Christian denominations has stayed constant and the numbers of people affiliating with non-Christian religions has increased.[3]

This slow down in the trend towards secularisation may be explained by younger generations being more ethnically diverse than older generations as the immigrant minority ethnic population in the UK are more religious on average than the White British population, with Pakistanis, Bangladeshis and Black Africans significantly more likely to assert the importance of their religion to their identity. However, it may be that these groups are showing similar patterns of intergenerational decline between generations,[4] with the 'second generation' (born in the UK to immigrant parents) being generally less religious than their parents – although Islam shows a higher level of intergenerational transmission compared to other religions.[5]

Published December 2014

⇨ The above information is reprinted with kind permission from HM Government. Please visit www.gov.uk for further information.

1 Ipsos MORI (2013) Generations [online] available from: http://www.ipsos-mori-generations.com

2 McAndrew, S. (2013) *Unpublished analysis of European Values Survey 1990, 1999 and 2009.* University of Manchester Institute for Social Change

3 Park, A. et al. Eds. (2013) *British Social Attitudes 30* NatCen Social Research [online]. Available from: http://www.bsa-30.natcen.ac.uk/media/37580/bsa30_full_report_final.pdf

4 Güveli, A. and Platt, L. (2011) Understanding the religious behaviour of Muslims in the Netherlands and the UK. *Sociology*, 45(6), 1008–1027.

5 Scourfield, J., Taylor, C., Moore, G., and Gilliat-Ray, S. (2012). The intergenerational transmission of Islam in England and Wales: Evidence from the Citizenship Survey. *Sociology*, 46(1), 91–108.

These are the world's most religious countries

The UK is one of the least religious countries in the world, according to a new study, but two thirds of the global population consider themselves to be religious.

By Raziye Akkoc

Across the world, two thirds of citizens believe they are a religious person but the UK is one of the least religious countries in the world, according to a new study.

Only 30 per cent of British people said they were religious compared with 53 per cent who said they were not a religious person. But only a small amount of Britons believed they were convinced atheists – 13 per cent.

The survey by WIN/Gallup International involved speaking face-to-face, on the telephone or online with nearly 64,000 people in 65 countries.

The most religious country was Thailand where 94 per cent of respondents said they were a religious person. Only one per cent said they were a convinced atheist.

Here are some of the other findings:

Young people are more religious than older adults

The findings showed that religion – far from heading towards a decline – was on course to thrive after two thirds of adults aged up to 34 considered themselves faithful.

The average for all other age groups was 60 per cent.

Jean-Marc Leger, president of WIN/Gallup International Association, said the survey showed the continued dominance of religion.

'[W]e see that the total number of people who consider themselves to be religious is actually relatively high. Furthermore, with the trend of an increasingly religious youth globally, we can assume that the number of people who consider themselves religious will only continue to increase.'

Religious people are a majority in all educational levels...

But 80 per cent of those with no education said they were religious compared with 60 per cent of secondary school and university-educated individuals.

The majority of the world's continents identify themselves as religious

The survey found that the majority of continents consider themselves to be a religious individual, except Australasia and Western Europe where 44 and 43 per cent of individuals said they were religious.

The survey comes after the Pew Research Center said last month that Islam would be the dominant religion globally in 2100.

In their study of the religious landscape in 2050, the researchers also said atheism would decline in 35 years across the world except in the West.

13 April 2015

⇨ The above information is reprinted with kind permission from *The Telegraph*. Please visit www.telegraph.co.uk for further information.

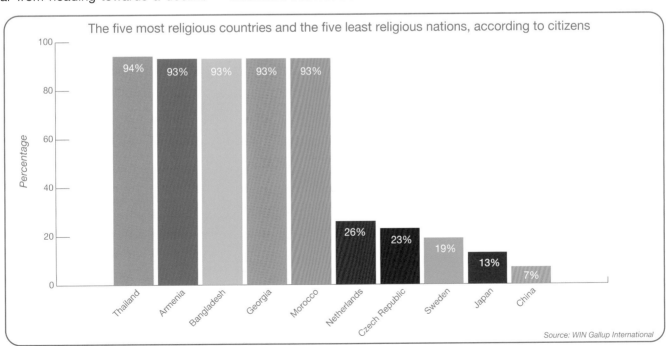

The five most religious countries and the five least religious nations, according to citizens

- Thailand: 94%
- Armenia: 93%
- Bangladesh: 93%
- Georgia: 93%
- Morocco: 93%
- Netherlands: 26%
- Czech Republic: 23%
- Sweden: 19%
- Japan: 13%
- China: 7%

Percentage (y-axis)

Source: WIN Gallup International

The Future of World Religions: Population Growth Projections, 2010–2050

Why Muslims are rising fastest and the unaffiliated are shrinking as a share of the world's population.

The religious profile of the world is rapidly changing, driven primarily by differences in fertility rates and the size of youth populations among the world's major religions, as well as by people switching faiths. Over the next four decades, Christians will remain the largest religious group, but Islam will grow faster than any other major religion. If current trends continue, by 2050:

⇨ The number of Muslims will nearly equal the number of Christians around the world.

⇨ Atheists, agnostics and other people who do not affiliate with any religion – though increasing in countries such as the US and France – will make up a declining share of the world's total population.

⇨ The global Buddhist population will be about the same size it was in 2010, while the Hindu and Jewish populations will be larger than they are today.

⇨ In Europe, Muslims will make up 10% of the overall population.

⇨ India will retain a Hindu majority but also will have the largest Muslim population of any country in the world, surpassing Indonesia.

⇨ In the US, Christians will decline from more than three-quarters of the population in 2010 to two-thirds in 2050, and Judaism will no longer be the largest non-Christian religion. Muslims will be more numerous in the US than people who identify as Jewish on the basis of religion.

⇨ Four out of every ten Christians in the world will live in sub-Saharan Africa.

These are among the global religious trends highlighted in new demographic projections by the Pew Research Center. The projections take into account the current size and geographic distribution of the world's major religions, age differences, fertility and mortality rates, international migration and patterns in conversion.

As of 2010, Christianity was by far the world's largest religion, with an estimated 2.2 billion adherents, nearly a third (31%) of all 6.9 billion people on Earth. Islam was second, with 1.6 billion adherents, or 23% of the global population.

If current demographic trends continue, however, Islam will nearly catch up by the middle of the 21st century. Between 2010 and 2050, the world's total population is expected to rise to 9.3 billion, a 35% increase. Over that same period, Muslims – a comparatively youthful population with high fertility rates – are projected to increase by 73%. The number of Christians also is projected to rise, but more slowly, at about the same rate (35%) as the global population overall.

As a result, according to the Pew Research projections, by 2050 there will be near parity between Muslims (2.8 billion, or 30% of the population) and Christians (2.9

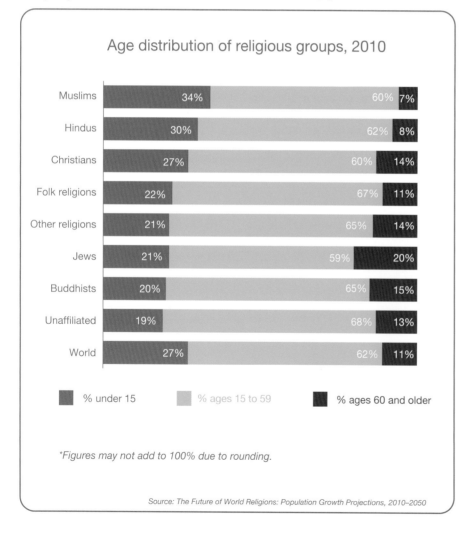

Age distribution of religious groups, 2010

	% under 15	% ages 15 to 59	% ages 60 and older
Muslims	34%	60%	7%
Hindus	30%	62%	8%
Christians	27%	60%	14%
Folk religions	22%	67%	11%
Other religions	21%	65%	14%
Jews	21%	59%	20%
Buddhists	20%	65%	15%
Unaffiliated	19%	68%	13%
World	27%	62%	11%

Figures may not add to 100% due to rounding.

Source: The Future of World Religions: Population Growth Projections, 2010–2050

billion, or 31%), possibly for the first time in history.

With the exception of Buddhists, all of the world's major religious groups are poised for at least some growth in absolute numbers in the coming decades. The global Buddhist population is expected to be fairly stable because of low fertility rates and ageing populations in countries such as China, Thailand and Japan.

Worldwide, the Hindu population is projected to rise by 34%, from a little over one billion to nearly 1.4 billion, roughly keeping pace with overall population growth. Jews, the smallest religious group for which separate projections were made, are expected to grow 16%, from a little less than 14 million in 2010 to 16.1 million worldwide in 2050.

Adherents of various folk religions – including African traditional religions, Chinese folk religions, Native American religions and Australian aboriginal religions – are projected to increase by 11%, from 405 million to nearly 450 million.

And all other religions combined – an umbrella category that includes Baha'is, Jains, Sikhs, Taoists and many smaller faiths – are projected to increase 6%, from a total of approximately 58 million to more than 61 million over the same period.

While growing in absolute size, however, folk religions, Judaism and 'other religions' (the umbrella category considered as a whole) will not keep pace with global population growth. Each of these groups is projected to make up a smaller percentage of the world's population in 2050 than it did in 2010.

Similarly, the religiously unaffiliated population is projected to shrink as a percentage of the global population, even though it will increase in absolute number. In 2010, censuses and surveys indicate, there were about 1.1 billion atheists, agnostics and people who do not identify with any particular religion. By 2050, the unaffiliated population is expected to exceed 1.2 billion. But, as a share of all the

people in the world, those with no religious affiliation are projected to decline from 16% in 2010 to 13% by the middle of this century.

At the same time, however, the unaffiliated are expected to continue to increase as a share of the population in much of Europe and North America. In the US, for example, the unaffiliated are projected to grow from an estimated 16% of the total population (including children) in 2010 to 26% in 2050.

As the example of the unaffiliated shows, there will be vivid geographic differences in patterns of religious growth in the coming decades. One of the main determinants of that future growth is where each group is geographically concentrated today. Religions with many adherents in developing countries – where birth rates are high, and infant mortality rates generally have been falling – are likely to grow quickly. Much of the worldwide growth of Islam and Christianity, for example, is expected to take place in sub-Saharan Africa. Today's religiously unaffiliated population, by contrast, is heavily concentrated in places with low fertility and ageing populations, such as Europe, North America, China and Japan.

Globally, Muslims have the highest fertility rate, an average of 3.1 children per woman – well above replacement level (2.1), the minimum typically needed to maintain a stable population. Christians are second, at 2.7 children per woman. Hindu fertility (2.4) is similar to the global average (2.5). Worldwide, Jewish fertility (2.3 children per woman) also is above replacement level. All the other groups have fertility levels too low to sustain their populations: folk religions (1.8 children per woman), other religions (1.7), the unaffiliated (1.7) and Buddhists (1.6).

Another important determinant of growth is the current age distribution of each religious group – whether its adherents are predominantly young, with their prime childbearing years still ahead, or older and largely past their childbearing years.

In 2010, more than a quarter of the world's total population (27%) was under the age of 15. But an even higher percentage of Muslims (34%) and Hindus (30%) were younger than 15, while the share of Christians under 15 matched the global average (27%). These bulging youth populations are among the reasons that Muslims are projected to grow faster than the world's overall population and that Hindus and Christians are projected to roughly keep pace with worldwide population growth.

All the remaining groups have smaller-than-average youth populations, and many of them have disproportionately large numbers of adherents over the age of 59. For example, 11% of the world's population was at least 60 years old in 2010. But fully 20% of Jews around the world are 60 or older, as are 15% of Buddhists, 14% of Christians, 14% of adherents of other religions (taken as a whole), 13% of the unaffiliated and 11% of adherents of folk religions. By contrast, just 7% of Muslims and 8% of Hindus are in this oldest age category.

In addition to fertility rates and age distributions, religious switching is likely to play a role in the growth of religious groups. But conversion patterns are complex and varied. In some countries, it is fairly common for adults to leave their childhood religion and switch to another faith. In others, changes in religious identity are rare, legally cumbersome or even illegal.

The Pew Research Center projections attempt to incorporate patterns in religious switching in 70 countries where surveys provide information on the number of people who say they no longer belong to the religious group in which they were raised. In the projection model, all directions of switching are possible, and they may be partially offsetting. In the US, for example, surveys find that some people who were raised with no religious affiliation have switched to become Christians, while some who grew up as Christians have switched to become unaffiliated. These types of patterns are projected to continue as future generations come of age.

Over the coming decades, Christians are expected to experience the largest net losses from switching. Globally, about 40 million people are projected to switch into Christianity, while 106 million are projected to leave, with most joining the ranks of the religiously unaffiliated.

All told, the unaffiliated are expected to add 97 million people and lose 36 million via switching, for a net gain of 61 million by 2050. Modest net gains through switching also are expected for Muslims (three million), adherents of folk religions (three million) and members of other religions (two million). Jews are expected to experience a net loss of about 300,000 people due to switching, while Buddhists are expected to lose nearly three million.

International migration is another factor that will influence the projected size of religious groups in various regions and countries.

Forecasting future migration patterns is difficult, because migration is often linked to government policies and international events that can change quickly. For this reason, many population projections do not include migration in their models. But working with researchers at the International Institute for Applied Systems Analysis in Laxenburg, Austria, the Pew Research Center has developed an innovative way of using data on past migration patterns to estimate the religious composition of migrant flows in the decades ahead.

In Europe, the Muslim share of the population is expected to increase from 5.9% in 2010 to 10.2% in 2050 when migration is taken into account along with other demographic factors that are driving population change, such as fertility rates and age. Without migration, the Muslim share of Europe's population in 2050 is projected to be nearly two percentage points lower (8.4%). In North America, the Hindu share of the population is expected to nearly double in the decades ahead, from 0.7% in 2010 to 1.3% in 2050, when migration is included in the projection models. Without migration, the Hindu share of the region's population would remain about the same (0.8%).

In the Middle East and North Africa, the continued migration of Christians into the six Gulf Cooperation Council (GCC) countries (Bahrain, Kuwait, Oman, Qatar, Saudi Arabia and the United Arab Emirates) is expected to offset the exodus of Christians from other countries in the region. If migration were not factored into the 2050 projections, the estimated Christian share of the region's population would drop below 3%. With migration factored in, however, the estimated Christian share is expected to be just above 3% (down from nearly 4% in 2010).

2 April 2015

⇨ The above information is reprinted with kind permission from the Pew Research Center. Please visit www.pewforum.org for further information.

Religion or belief in the workplace: an explanation of recent European Court of Human Rights judgments

In January 2013, the European Court of Human Rights (the Court) published its judgment in four combined cases about religious rights in the workplace. The cases are: Eweida and Chaplin v. the United Kingdom and Ladele and McFarlane v. the United Kingdom. The cases were brought by Christians, but the implications of the judgment apply to employees with any religion or belief, or none. The judgment affects employer responsibilities for policies and practices affecting religion or belief rights in the workplace, the rights of employees (including job applicants) and the rights of customers or service users.

What laws protect rights to religion or belief?

The Equality Act 2010 prohibits unlawful harassment, victimisation and direct and indirect discrimination at work based on religion or belief. The law concerning indirect discrimination was most relevant in these cases when they were considered by the domestic courts/tribunals. Moreover, since April 2011, section 149 of the Equality Act 2010 requires public authorities when exercising their functions to give due regard to eliminating prohibited conduct, advancing equality of opportunity and fostering good relations. These positive obligations, commonly known as the public sector equality duty, cover eight protected characteristics including religion or belief.

Article 9 of the European Convention on Human Rights (incorporated into UK law through the Human Rights Act 1998) provides unqualified protection for freedom of thought, conscience and religion. It also provides protection for the right to express or manifest religion or belief in worship, teaching, practice and observance, but, because manifestation by one person of his or her belief may have an impact on others, these rights are qualified and can be restricted in certain circumstances. Article 9 is complemented by Article 14 of the European Convention on Human Rights, which requires that people enjoy all the rights under the Convention without discrimination. Article 14 is not a free-standing right; it can only operate when another Convention right is engaged.

Religion or belief manifestation rights under Article 9 can be limited, but any limitation must be prescribed by law and necessary in a democratic society in the interests of public safety, the protection of public order, health or morals, or the protection of the rights and freedoms of others. Indirect discrimination based on religion or belief under the Equality Act 2010 or interferences with Article 14 anti-discrimination rights can be justified if this is a proportionate means of achieving a legitimate aim.

What were the cases about?

Eweida and Chaplin were both prevented by their employers' dress codes from wearing a visible cross/crucifix when in uniform at work. The majority of the European Court of Human Rights decided that their religious rights at work needed to be balanced against other considerations. In the case of Eweida, an airline check-in officer, they found that her Article 9 right to manifest her belief was unjustifiably breached. The domestic courts gave too much weight to the employer's legitimate need to project a corporate image and not enough weight to the employee's right to wear a visible cross, which did not adversely affect that corporate image. In the case of Chaplin, a nurse, the Court unanimously concluded that the health and safety of staff and patients outweighed the right of the employee to wear a visible crucifix on a chain around her neck. The employer's decision interfered with her Article 9 rights, but it was justifiable on health and safety grounds.

Ladele and McFarlane both objected, due to their religious beliefs about marriage and sexual relationships, to carrying out certain work duties in respect of same-sex couples. The European Court of Human Rights found against both of them. In Ladele, a registrar who refused to perform civil partnerships and was ultimately dismissed, the majority of the Court found that the employer's application of the corporate 'equality and dignity' policy to refuse to exempt an employee from particular duties, was within the range of permissible choices available to the employer, and the domestic courts had not exceeded the wide discretion given to them when determining this case which involved striking a balance between competing Convention rights. In reaching that conclusion, the majority of the Court did not accept the employee's argument that the employer should have accommodated her conscientious objection.

In McFarlane, a counsellor who refused to offer psycho-sexual therapy to same-sex couples contrary to his employer's non-discrimination policy and was dismissed, the Court unanimously decided that a fair balance was struck between the competing interests at stake. The most important factor for the Court was that the employer's action was intended to secure the implementation of its policy of providing a service without discrimination. Accordingly, although the Court recognised that the loss of a job was a severe sanction with grave consequences, it concluded the State had not exceeded the wide discretion it enjoys to determine the right balance between manifesting religious belief and protecting the rights of others.

What legal changes does this judgment make?

Until recently, the European Court of Human Rights and our domestic courts tended to take the view that a practice was protected under Article 9 only if it was required by the particular religion or belief. The new judgment confirms that a practice or manifestation motivated, influenced or inspired by religion or belief, and which is sufficiently linked to the religion or belief will be protected, regardless of whether it is a mandatory requirement of the religion or belief. Both Eweida and Chaplin could show their wish to wear a cross/crucifix visibly at work was genuine and motivated by a desire to bear witness to their Christian faith although neither claimed that it was a requirement of their religion. The Court considered that this behaviour was a manifestation of religious belief, attracting the protection of Article 9. It should now be easier for individuals to establish Article 9 rights to manifest religion or belief, placing greater focus on the next stage of the decision-making process, which is to assess whether any interference with such rights is justifiable.

In the past, employees in similar situations to Eweida, Chaplin, Ladele and McFarlane may have been expected to resign and look for other jobs if they wished to observe their religion or belief in the workplace.

There have been legal cases in the past where an individual's right to manifest their religion or belief has been limited on this basis.

The European Court of Human Rights concluded that this approach could not be followed rigidly. The new judgment means that the courts cannot simply dismiss a case because of the possibility of changing jobs to other employment that allows the religious observance. Instead, this possibility should be a relevant factor, to be weighed amongst others, when considering whether or not the restriction is proportionate.

The judgment means that courts will now give more attention to deciding whether restrictions on religious rights in the workplace are appropriate and necessary. Some relevant considerations for employers include the need to:

⇨ Take a balanced view of the religion or belief needs of the employee

⇨ Review policies and practices causing problems for employees related to religion or belief, ensuring employees are not subjected to a detriment at work whilst this happens

⇨ Consider the impact that meeting those needs has on other employees

⇨ Consider the impact that meeting those needs has on customers, and

⇨ Consider whether the aim they are pursuing is legitimate and, if so, whether it is being pursued by proportionate means.

The courts will assess the weight of each type of relevant consideration to determine where the right balance lies in the particular circumstances of each case. The Commission's companion guide helps to explain how employers can do this in practice, enabling them to comply with the judgment when recognising and managing the expression of religion or belief in the workplace.

5 September 2014

Religion study finds believers under pressure in workplace – echoing case of Devon nurse Shirley Chaplin

Religious employees feel under pressure to keep their beliefs and faith symbols hidden while at work, according to a study by the equality watchdog.

Those who were openly Christian complained of being mocked as bigots, while Jewish and Muslim workers reported finding it hard to get time off work for religious reasons, the research by the Equality and Human Rights Commission found.

Meanwhile, atheists and humanists who responded to the survey said they had experienced unwanted conversion attempts and felt excluded from company events held in religious buildings.

And children of Christian parents were said to have been 'ridiculed' for their beliefs, while humanist parents claimed their youngsters had also been mocked – including one told they did not deserve Christmas presents as they did not believe in God.

The research, based on 2,483 responses from individuals and organisations, comes as the watchdog prepares a report into laws protecting religious freedoms and looks to issue guidelines for employers and the public.

The findings come three years after a nurse who lost a landmark European legal battle called on David Cameron to change a law preventing religious symbols being worn at work.

Judges at the European Court of Human Rights (ECHR) ruled Shirley Chaplin was not allowed to wear a crucifix to work as it would breach health and safety laws, despite the fact she had worn it for 30 years.

Mrs Chaplin called on the Prime Minister to fulfil a promise to change the law on religious objects in the workplace, saying he should 'actually do it'.

At the time, she said: 'It seems ridiculous to me – I wore it (the crucifix) on my confirmation when I was 16, I've been a nurse since 1978.

'I've worn it without incident, I've nursed a very wide range of patients, I've been bitten, I've been scratched, I've had computers thrown at me, but no one has ever, ever grabbed my crucifix.'

The Bishop of Exeter Reverend Michael Langrish, speaking after the ruling in 2013, said he was 'disappointed' by the verdict, which also saw a British Airways employee win her discrimination case for wearing a cross.

'The issue at stake is how to balance the issue of equality and diversity in the framework of law.

'The balance is currently against rights of conscience and rights of faith,' he said.

Mark Hammond, CEO of the Equality and Human Rights Commission, today said: 'How the law deals with religion and other beliefs in work, in providing services and in public debate has become a matter of considerable controversy.

'What we found from the thousands of responses we received was a complex picture of different opinions and experiences. However, what came out strongly was the widespread confusion about the law, leading to some resentment and tensions between groups and anxiety for employers who fear falling foul of what they see as complicated equality and human rights legislation.

'We also found examples of organisations which had taken a constructive approach to dealing with issues of religion or belief, with employees providing positive experiences of diverse and inclusive workplaces.'

Other examples cited by people who responded include a Catholic who was unable to wear a crucifix or rosary while others had nose rings and piercings and a law firm manager who faced objections to organising a Christmas party as it promoted religion.

Some Christian businesses reported being 'in turmoil' over whether actions might breach the Equality Act, aimed at preventing discrimination in the workplace.

Mr Hammond added: 'We'll use this evidence as we examine how effective the law is in this area and develop guidance which we hope will help everyone address some of the issues which have come out of the consultation.'

Andrea Williams, chief executive of the Christian Legal Centre speaking of Shirley Chaplin's case in an interview with Christian Concern published on Saturday, said: 'Before elections, political leaders may talk about Britain being a Christian country and how valued the contribution of the church is. They may even say that "faith should not be left at the door". But if those that want to represent us are really serious, what we need now are clear commitments from party leaders to institute proper protections for Christian conscience and expression. And after the election we need speedy and concrete action to that end.

'Let's not forget that it was this Coalition Government that told the European Court of Human Rights, in the case of nurse Shirley Chaplin, that the wearing of the cross is not a recognisable form of practising the Christian faith and that if someone's freedom of religion is not sufficiently protected they are free to resign and find employment elsewhere.'

Terry Sanderson is president of the National Secular Society, speaking of Christian claims against discrimination, said: 'It is trying to create a climate that will persuade politicians that the Equality Act needs to be changed to give them the right to refuse goods and services to people they believe don't live by biblical standards.

'They want the right not just to hold their beliefs, but to promote them in the workplace, to impose them on customers and service users and to have special privileges that are denied to everyone else.'

The NatCen Social Research carried out the research of 2,483 people and organisations between August and October 2014 on behalf of the Commission. The majority of respondents were Christian (1,030) followed by atheists (188). Other faiths were included in smaller numbers.

12 March 2015

⇨ The above information is reprinted with kind permission from the Press Association. Please visit www. pressassociation.com for further information.

God's work? The battle over religious belief in the office

THE CONVERSATION

*This article is from **The Conversation.***

By Scott Taylor, Reader in Leadership & Organization Studies at University of Birmingham

What do you want from your employer at Easter? A chocolate egg? A big slice of Simnel cake? Some time off? An invitation to attend a Christian church service? Or nothing at all, because you don't find Easter meaningful and would rather your workplace was entirely secular?

Managerial responses to the cultural complexity of religious diversity range from following highly structured legal guidance to informal acceptance of contemporary pluralism by working around staff beliefs. There are legal frameworks in most countries to either protect or exclude religious belief from workplaces. But how these are worked out in practice creates considerable controversy. And when we consider religious belief alongside sexual orientation or ethnicity, then we're almost certain of dispute.

So what happens if you are required to follow a specific belief system at work? If you're an Anglican priest, then it shouldn't cause you a problem to believe in God as part of the employment relationship. Is it reasonable, though, for legally secular companies to impose religious beliefs on workers? And what if managers or owners in an organisation expect you to refuse to provide services to certain people because, from a specific religious perspective, their sexualities are somehow wrong?

The Protestant work ethic

Removing religion from the workplace is extremely difficult, if not impossible. Classical sociologist Max Weber wasn't the first to note the considerable influence religious belief can have on work and workplaces in the early 1900s. He did open up a lively debate, though, that continues more than 100 years later.

Weber's thesis was superficially simple – that Protestantism strongly influenced the development of capitalism in Western Europe and North America. Weber argued that this was especially clear in the Calvinist doctrine of doing work to the glory of God, combined with exhortations to live frugally. The combination of rational hard work and retention of wages or profits resulted in earnings that could be invested in more productive enterprises – hence capitalism based on growth.

Through Weber's seminal work, religion explains the most significant economic change of modernity, in a way that is intuitively appealing. It can be used to explain the enduring puzzle of why some people work harder than others, how some people accumulate more wealth, and why different parts of the world developed economically at different moments.

Weber's argument, data and conclusions have all been repeatedly challenged. Nonetheless, the notion of a religious work ethic is still with us in a range of forms – not necessarily Christian or underpinned by any religion. North American researchers in business schools propose a contemporary form when they argue that the promotion of spirituality in the workplace can result in higher productivity or more ethical leadership.

Equality and religion

Is that what we want from employers, though – to be guided as to what we should believe about the world in such a fundamental way, to be seen as a better employee? That direction results in Josiah Wedgwood encouraging potters to convert to Methodism so that he can rely on them to turn up to work sober on

Monday morning and stay until the end of the day, making it possible to mechanise a production process that had been based on rule of thumb and the need to work.

The industrialist William Lever appointed a pliable Anglican vicar to preach the virtues of obedience to managers in the only church in his purpose-built town at Port Sunlight. More recently, managers at Tyson Foods and Walmart have encouraged employees to honour God, as a core company value. Is this what we look for at work?

Of course, all organisations generate a culture – which religious belief will inevitably be a part of. More disciplinary or 'strong' cultures were the preferred option for managers for some time, as it was said to encourage a conformity that would be helpful for discipline. But trends toward workplace diversity and inclusion have challenged the idea of a mono-culture that creates somewhat robotic employees, often of one ethnic type or one gender.

A recent rise in legislation, however, is forcing company owners and managers to deal with the issue of religion at work. The EU-inspired British Equality Act of 2010 brought together a series of smaller pieces of workplace-related legislation, such as the Sexual Orientation and Religious Belief Act of 2003, to provide a coherent anti-discrimination equal-treatment guidance for most areas of employment. But the wrangles continue.

Controversy to be continued

It is clear already from case law that religion is likely to be the most controversial aspect of promoting equality, both in employment and in the provision of services. Something as mundane as an order for a decorated cake can create new case law. A bakery in Northern Ireland has been accused of discrimination against a gay man for refusing to make a 'gay cake' on religious grounds – judgement is currently reserved, but it's sure that some will be unhappy whatever the outcome.

Meanwhile in the US, a series of states are attempting to legislate in favour of discrimination against LGBT people, if a religious freedom argument is given for it. This has led to a somewhat incongruous statement from Asda's owner Walmart in favour of diversity, opposing the debated religious freedom bill. Lest we forget, this Walmart is one of the most prominently featured organisations on Corporate Watch, especially for systematic racial and gender discrimination.

More convincingly, Apple's Tim Cook has begun to speak publicly on this issue, on his own behalf and with the power of Apple behind him.

Religious belief (or lack of it – the New Atheist movement can be as dogmatic and doctrinaire as the most disciplinary of religions) continues to occupy a uniquely controversial position in societies around the world. Opponents claim it causes conflict and social inequality; believers assert that life without it is constrained and meaningless. Both make claims to freedom of expression and the need for freedom from others' beliefs.

Meanwhile, the workplace is a key site for religion's expression and constraint – as an individual and as a means of expressing corporate identity. As the legal system is challenged and revised, we can expect many more individual controversies and corporate interventions to come.

2 April 2015

⇨ The above information is reprinted with kind permission from *The Conversation*. Please visit www. theconversation.com for further information.

Religious education and the law

RE is a statutory part of the basic curriculum and all maintained schools by law and academies by virtue of their funding agreement must provide RE for all children attending school.

Parents have the right to withdraw their child from all or any part of RE. This includes parents whose children attend a faith school. If pupils are withdrawn from RE, schools have a duty to supervise them, though not to provide additional or alternative teaching.

RE is the only statutory subject that is not part of the National Curriculum.

Community schools and voluntary controlled faith schools follow a locally agreed syllabus drawn up by local committees (known as Standing Advisory Council on Religious Education, or SACRE) comprising of teachers, local churches, faith groups and the local authority.

In voluntary aided faith schools the syllabus is a matter for the governing body to decide – and may be of denominational character. This means that a significant number of state funded 'faith schools' are permitted to teach RE from a selective, exclusive or confessional viewpoint, more analogous to religious instruction than education.

As a condition of their funding agreements, all academies and free schools have to provide RE for their pupils. The type of RE specified in the funding agreement depends on whether or not the academy has a religious designation, and for converter academies, on whether the predecessor school was a voluntary controlled (VC), voluntary aided (VA) or foundation school.

Other than for academies where the predecessor school was a VC or foundation school, the model funding agreement specifies that an academy with a religious designation must provide RE in accordance with the tenets of the particular faith of the school. They may, in addition, provide RE that is in line with a locally agreed syllabus and teach about other faiths if they choose.

⇨ The above information is reprinted with kind permission from the National Secular Society. Please visit www. secularism.org.uk for further information.

Why do schools sideline religious education?

RE taught me valuable skills, but it still isn't taken seriously in schools, writes a student blogger.

By Saema Jaffer

Religious education just isn't taken seriously at school. It is undervalued and unappreciated. Merged with citizenship and social studies, it sits huddled in a corner at the edge of the humanities office. But it can teach students valuable ways of thinking that help at university and later on in life too.

Religious education (RE) is so easily ignored that one of the schools I went to didn't even give the subject its own teachers, instead making do with borrowed staff from health and social care, sociology and PE.

Yet every day we're surrounded by issues that require us to look at events from the perspective of others – a key skill that you learn through RE. But because of the way RE is treated, the subject is often seen as irrelevant.

'Why do we have to learn this?' we whined in every subject within ten minutes of starting the lesson, 'what use will this be in the real world?'

While other subjects were staunchly defended at school, RE was always seen as a tertiary subject. The maths teacher told us that it taught us to think logically; to use a step-by-step approach in working through problems. The geography teacher would insist his subject was useful: his lessons increased our understanding of global warming and the impact of our consumerism on the planet.

But from RE, we never had an answer. 'Because the school says it's compulsory' was the closest we ever got. One teacher even shrugged in response to the question at my school. All this despite the fact that RE lessons were probably the closest we ever came to understanding the ideas that shaped our world.

After all, it was in RE, not history, where I first learnt the principles underpinning Gandhi's struggles and Martin Luther King's protests. It was also in RE where we were credited for thinking critically rather than memorising facts, for articulating opinions and backing up our views and for taking time to consider an issue from a different perspective. These are skills we use at university and in our everyday lives.

Law student Mohammed-Husnain says: '[Because of RE] I believe I have become a better communicator as a whole. It now means I find it easier assessing both sides of an argument before coming to a conclusion.'

The lessons taught in RE are especially necessary after leaving school, as we meet people from different backgrounds, traditions and religious beliefs from across the world.

The underestimated importance of RE is also that it helps overcome prejudices and negative stereotypes. If people have a better understanding of other faiths, they're less likely to be dismissive of issues that don't concern them directly. Better still, it promotes integration and a stronger sense of community.

It's about time that schools – and students – realised the importance of religious education.

15 January 2014

⇨ The above information is reprinted with kind permission from *The Guardian*. Please visit www.theguardian.com for further information.

Ending Christian assembly: let's open our eyes to the value of collective worship in schools

THE CONVERSATION

This article is from **The Conversation.**

By Brian Gates, Emeritus Professor of Religion, Ethics & Education at University of Cumbria

Challenges from parents and teachers to the law requiring an act of collective worship in schools are not new. Now the National Governors' Association has called for Christian assemblies in non-religious state schools to be scrapped.

But while the time is ripe for a re-engagement with the law, ironically, collective worship is important to the current debate about British values in education.

Collective worship can be a formative learning experience for both British and global values. It can ramify across a whole school curriculum and, when accompanied by the critical intelligence promoted by good religious education, contribute hugely to moral discernment.

'Worship' (or worthship) is all about 'attributing worth to' something. An imaginative interpretation of collective worship is an opportunity for a school to gather round and explore the deepest beliefs and values which inform the communities that feed into it. That includes exposure to stories and music, anniversaries and festivals, visual imagery and performance. These may be celebrating, regretting or rebuking, but they will all be set within the horizons of a common wealth which is Christian, and secular and multi-faith.

40 years of looking for an alternative

Reistance to the requirement for collective worship surfaced in 1975 in reports from the then Schools Council and John Hull's book *School Worship: An Obituary*. It was also there in discussions ahead of the 1988 Education Reform Act. But politicians were reluctant to abandon the legal requirement. This was because a minority of them believed that what happened in schools should be the same as in any local church on a Sunday. For many more politicians it was a recognition that the provision remained overwhelmingly popular according to repeated opinion polls.

There was a major attempt to arrive at an alternative arrangement in the mid-1990s. It took the form of a national consultation by the Inter Faith Network for the UK, the National Associations of Standing Advisory Councils for Religious Education (SACREs), and the Religious Education Council of England and Wales. This produced large-scale consensus, but the lack of total unanimity was enough to excuse government inaction.

In 2003, Charles Clarke, when he was Secretary of State for Education, promised that he would pick up on this once the development of a National Framework for Religious Education was completed. It was in 2004, but by then Clarke had been moved on to the Home Office.

It is time for another rethink. What sort is a different matter and it would be wise to reflect carefully on the desirable outcomes of any changes.

The law as it stands

Contrary to impressions conveyed in the media, the current legal prescription, which was introduced in 1988 and stands to this day, is both more sophisticated and more flexible than ephemeral headlines allow. It states that:

⇨ Worship should be 'collective' not 'corporate'. Corporate worship is an activity distinctive to a community of believers gathering to express their shared faith. Collective worship

is an activity expressive of the religious beliefs of some but not all of those present. Arguably, the former might be appropriate in some 'schools of a religious character', such as faith schools, but certainly not in all other state-funded schools. There, collective worship is what is legally specified.

⇨ 'Wholly or mainly of a broadly Christian character'. This convoluted phrase was introduced into the 1988 Education Reform Act to indicate that Christian beliefs and values are an important part of a school's constitution, reflecting that of the nation. It was also introduced to ensure that head teachers and governors could also have the professional discretion to be attentive to other mainstream beliefs and values.

'Wholly broadly Christian' expressly ruled out any denominational loadings. 'Mainly' permitted just under half to attend to other beliefs and values. This ruling sits alongside the requirement that religious education teaching must include the other principal religions of the UK as well as Christianity. More than 25 years ago the same Education Act (section 8) made it illegal to ignore Muslim traditions, as well as those of other faiths. Those faiths should deservedly include that of the humanist community – a legal change now well worth considering.

⇨ 'Age, aptitude and family background'. The law prescribes that, in arriving at the form of collective worship appropriate to the school, the headteacher must give careful consideration to the family backgrounds of pupils and also to their age and aptitude. When this was introduced back in 1988, schools were then advised by local authorities that assemblies could be variable in composition – such as divided up by year group or class.

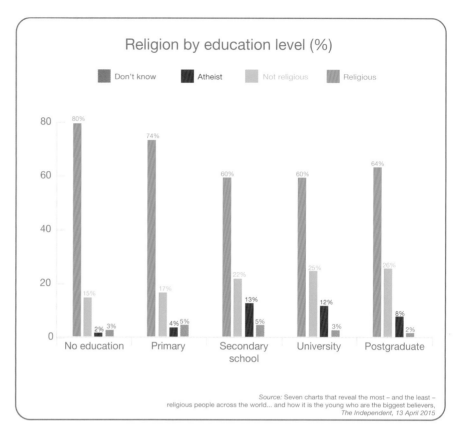

Religion by education level (%)

Source: Seven charts that reveal the most – and the least – religious people across the world... and how it is the young who are the biggest believers, *The Independent*, 13 April 2015

⇨ 'Conscience clause'. This gives parents the right to withdraw their sons and daughters from RE and collective worship on conscience grounds. But good educational practice should make this unnecessary.

Government should step up

Any re-engagement with the issue of collective worship should properly involve much more than a shift in these legal wordings. One issue is the need, confirmed by the 2011 Census, to include humanist affirmations. Another is that of how to ensure that teachers and governors have the confidence and competence to work responsibly with religious diversity.

In practice, the assembling tradition is stronger in primary than secondary schools. And legal requirements regarding provision for daily collective worship, like those for effective religious education, have for many years been commonly ignored. Once upon a time, the entire school community would have been involved (minus conscientious objectors). Now, alongside the pupils, it is more usually only those teachers with designated responsibility.

Collective worship is neglected in initial teacher education and training, as it is in the further professional development, including that of head teachers. As with religious education, government ministers and the department of education have ignored evidence of underprovision from many quarters, even Ofsted.

But as the education community is being asked to look deep into its role in promoting religious tolerance in a multi-faith Britain, perhaps the Government should be more attentive to the fundamental aim that by the completion of formal education, young people are not only literate and numerate but also religiate. That's actually what the national religious education tradition is properly all about: the education of conscience.

3 July 2014

⇨ The above information is reprinted with kind permission from *The Conversation*. Please visit www.theconversation.com for further information.

© *The Conversation Trust 2015*

Religious Freedom in the World Report – 2014

At-a-glance findings.

(Period under review: October 2012 to June 2014)

1. Of the 196 countries in the world, 81 countries – or 41 per cent – are identified as places where religious freedom is impaired (classified as 'high' or 'medium') or is in decline.

2. A total of 35 countries – or 18 per cent – were classified as having some religious freedom issues that are 'of concern', but with no deterioration in their status.

3. The remaining 80 countries – or 41 per cent – indicated no concerns regarding religious freedom. The report found no regular or systemic religious freedom violations in these nations.

4. Where there has been a change concerning religious freedom, that change has almost always been for the worse. In the 196 countries analysed, change for the better is noted in only six countries. Deteriorating conditions are recorded in 55 countries (or 28 per cent).

5. Even in the six countries where some improvements have been noted, four – Iran, United Arab Emirates, Cuba and Qatar – remain classified as places of 'high' or 'medium' persecution. Zimbabwe and Taiwan are classified 'of concern' and 'low' respectively.

6. In total, 20 countries are designated as 'high' with regard to lack of religious freedom.

- Of these, 14 experience religious persecution linked to extremist Islam. These are: Afghanistan, Central African Republic, Egypt, Iran, Iraq, Libya, Maldives, Nigeria, Pakistan, Saudi Arabia, Somalia, Sudan, Syria and Yemen.

- In the remaining six countries, religious persecution is linked to authoritarian regimes. These are: Burma (Myanmar), China, Eritrea, North Korea, Azerbaijan and Uzbekistan.

Based on these findings, the report concludes:

7. In the period under review, global religious freedom entered a period of serious decline.

8. The impression given by global media headlines of a rising tide of persecution aimed at marginalised religious communities is supported by this research.

9. Muslim countries predominate in the list of states with the most serious religious freedom violations.

10. Religious freedom is in decline in Western countries that are predominantly or historically Christian. Two principal factors explain this. First, there is disagreement over the role to be played by religion in the 'public square'. Second, openness to religious freedom is under threat from increasing societal concern about extremism.

11. Christians remain the most persecuted religious minority, due partly to their wide geographic spread and high relative numbers. However, Muslims are also experiencing a serious degree of persecution and discrimination, both at the hands of other Muslims and from authoritarian governments.

12. Jews in Western Europe are subject to violence and other abuse that is generally low-level. However, such problems have grown, prompting increased emigration to Israel.

13. Some positive signs of religious co-operation were identified, but these were often the result of local initiatives rather than progress at a national level.

14. The persecution of long-established religious minorities, and the rise of mono-confessional states, is resulting in exceptionally high population displacements that contribute to the worldwide refugee crisis.

15. The countries of Western Europe, which until recent decades were overwhelmingly Christian and racially homogenous, are becoming more like the multi-confessional and diverse societies of the Middle East. This is generating tensions, both political and social.

16. The rise of 'religious illiteracy' among both Western policy makers and the international media is hampering productive dialogue and effective policy making.

17. We conclude that, to reverse the disturbing trends identified in this Report, responsibility for combatting violence and persecution rests, first and foremost, within religious communities themselves. The necessity for all religious leaders to loudly proclaim their opposition to religiously-inspired violence, and to re-affirm their support for religious tolerance, is becoming ever more urgent.

Published in 2014

⇨ The above information is reprinted with kind permission from Aid to the Church in Need, UK. Please visit www.acnuk.org for further information.

The Freedom of Thought 2014: a global report on discrimination against Humanists, Atheists and the non-religious; their human tights and legal status

An extract from the Introduction of the Freedom of Thought report...

By the International Humanist and Ethical Union

A secularising world

Atheists (those who do not believe in any god), and humanists (those who embrace a morality centred on human welfare and human flourishing that does not appeal to any supernatural source), and others who consider themselves non-religious, are a large and growing population across the world. A detailed survey in 2012 revealed that religious people make up 59% of the world population, while those who identify as 'atheist' make up 13%, and an additional 23% identify as 'not religious' (while not self-identifying as 'atheist'). The report by the WIN-Gallup International Association is in line with other recent global surveys. It shows that atheism and the non-religious population are growing rapidly – religion dropped by 9% and atheism rose by 3% between 2005 and 2012 – and that religion declines in proportion to the rise in education and personal income, which is a trend that looks set to continue.

Freedom of thought and belief

The right to freedom of thought, conscience, religion or belief protects the individual conscience of every human being. This right was first stated by the global community in 1948 in Article 18 of the Universal Declaration of Human Rights. It states:

'Everyone has the right to freedom of thought, conscience and religion; this right includes freedom to change his religion or belief, and freedom, either alone or in community with others and in public or private, to manifest his religion or belief in teaching, practice, worship and observance.'

Article 18, Universal Declaration of Human Rights

This simple but powerful statement of the right to freedom of religion or belief was given the force of international law by Article 18 of the International Covenant on Civil and Political Rights in 1976. Then in 1981 it was given broader application and detail by the UN Declaration on the Elimination of All Forms of Intolerance and of Discrimination Based on Religion or Belief.

Just as freedom of thought, conscience, religion or belief protects the right of the individual to follow a religion, it also protects the right to reject any religion or belief, to identify as humanist or atheist, and to manifest non-religious convictions through expression, teaching and practice. As the United Nations Human Rights Committee explains (General Comment 22):

1. The right to freedom of thought, conscience and religion (which includes the freedom to hold beliefs) in article 18.1 is far-reaching and profound; it encompasses freedom of thought on all matters, personal conviction and the commitment to religion or belief, whether manifested individually or in community with others....

2. Article 18 protects theistic, non-theistic and atheistic beliefs, as well as the right not to profess any religion or belief. The terms 'belief' and 'religion' are to be broadly construed. Article 18 is not limited in its application to traditional religions or to religions and beliefs with institutional characteristics or practices analogous to those of traditional religions.'

Thus, it is not necessary to describe atheism as a religion, or as analogous to religion, to guarantee atheists the same protection as religious believers. On the contrary, atheism and theism are protected equally as manifestations of the fundamental right to freedom of thought and conscience.

Religious believers and non-believers are equal in human rights because they are all human, irrespective of their religion or beliefs. Just as the profession of religion is protected as a manifestation of belief and conscience, so is the atheist's criticism of religious beliefs and practices. Just as speaking in support of one's religious convictions and moral values can be of fundamental meaning and importance to the individual, so can advocating core humanist values of democracy, freedom, rationalism and human rights, or advocating secularism, or speaking out in opposition to religious beliefs, practices and authorities, or in support of atheist beliefs. After all, as the United Nations says, 'religion or belief, for anyone who professes either, is one of the fundamental elements in his conception of life' (UN Declaration on the Elimination of All Forms of Intolerance and of Discrimination Based on Religion or Belief).

Article 18 protects atheists qua atheists: it protects atheists' right to be atheist and to manifest their atheist beliefs – and non-beliefs – in public as well as in private, in teaching as well as in practice. The right to freedom of religion or belief is therefore central to our examination of the status of atheists and other non-religious people around the world. But there are other rights that are necessary for people to express their conscience, thoughts and beliefs.

Other rights and freedoms

The right to freedom of expression is, obviously, necessary for people to express their beliefs, but also to explore and exchange ideas. As stated by Article 19 of the Universal Declaration of Human Rights, the right to freedom of expression includes the right to share ideas and, crucially, the freedom of the media that is necessary for the free exchange of opinions as well as news:

'Everyone has the right to freedom of opinion and expression; this right includes freedom to hold opinions without interference and to seek, receive and impart information and ideas through any media and regardless of frontiers.'

– Article 19, Universal Declaration of Human Rights

In addition to expressing their thoughts through private discussion – or public media – people also have the right to associate with others who share those beliefs, and to express their thoughts at meetings, including public assemblies and demonstrations. These rights are protected by Article 20 of the Universal Declaration of Human Rights: 'Everyone has the right to freedom of peaceful assembly and association' (Article 20).

It's no coincidence that these three rights are stated together in the Universal Declaration of Human Rights: Articles 18, 19 and 20 are intertwined with each other, and generally stand or fall together. Our survey therefore looks at violations to the freedoms of expression, assembly and association, as well as freedom of religion or belief, to show how non-religious people are prevented from, or persecuted for, expressing their atheist ideas or humanist values.

The countries with the worst records on freedom of thought are usually the countries with the worst records on human rights overall. This is no coincidence: when thought is a crime, no other freedom can long survive.

Published in 2014

⇨ The above information is reprinted with kind permission from the International Humanist and Ethical Union (IHEU). Please visit http://freethoughtreport.com for further information and to read the report in full.

Hate speech, freedom of expression and freedom of religion: a dialogue

The relationship between hate speech, freedom of expression, freedom of religion and belief, and religious intolerance is politically fraught and legally complex. To provide clarity, this note takes the form of a dialogue: the dialogue is fictional, of course, but the questions are typical of those posed and argued both in public discourse and in formal legal and political settings. The issues discussed in this note intersect and overlap with other controversies. Particularly: (a) wider questions of freedom of expression, racism and the like. And (b) other debates within freedom of expression and freedom of religion or belief, including those on religious symbols in schools, wearing of religious dress (crucifixes, veils etc.), registration of religious sects, etc.

Are freedom of expression and freedom of religion in conflict?

It sometimes seems that way. Extreme speech can challenge and offend individuals' intimately-held religious beliefs and convictions. The reactions to cartoons satirising the prophet Muhammad, to burnings of the Koran, and to offensive anti-Islam videos can make it appear that an intractable conflict exists. And it's not just Islam and Muslims affected: many of the cases taken to the European Court of Human Rights (ECtHR) and communicated to the UN Human Rights Committee concern other beliefs, including Christianity and Judaism. Though in recent years, the most high profile cases causing the most international political controversy have tended to focus on intolerance against Islam, not least given the violent reaction by some people to some such instances of intolerance.

So that proves my point?

Not quite. Freedom of expression (FoE) certainly deals with speech and other forms of expression, and freedom of religion or belief (FoRB) deals with religion. Although these concepts may clash, a human rights perspective shows that FoE and FoRB can and should be complementary, and indeed mutually reinforcing. Many actions – e.g. to manifest one's religion – are protected by both FoE and FoRB. And there is as much potential for tension between two individuals' right to FoRB (or FoE) as there is between one person's right to FoE and another's right to FoRB.

What do you mean by a 'human rights perspective'?

One that is grounded in the actual text of legally-binding international human rights treaties, rather than abstract rights and wrongs. And also in relevant non-legally-binding political commitments made by States, e.g. in UN General Assembly and Human Rights Council declarations and resolutions. At the international level the relevant international human rights treaty is the International Covenant on Civil and Political Rights (ICCPR):

Article 18

1. Everyone shall have the right to freedom of thought, conscience and religion. This right shall include freedom to have or to adopt a religion or belief of his choice, and freedom, either individually or in community with others and in public or private, to manifest his religion or belief in worship, observance, practice and teaching.

2. No one shall be subject to coercion which would impair his freedom to have or to adopt a religion or belief of his choice.

3. Freedom to manifest one's religion or beliefs may be subject only to such limitations as are prescribed by law and are necessary to protect public safety, order, health, or morals or the fundamental rights and freedoms of others.

Article 19

1. Everyone shall have the right to hold opinions without interference.

2. Everyone shall have the right to freedom of expression; this right shall include freedom to seek, receive and impart information and ideas of all kinds, regardless of frontiers, either orally, in writing or in print, in the form of art, or through any other media of his choice.

3. The exercise of the rights provided for in paragraph 2 of this article carries with it special duties and responsibilities. It may therefore be subject to certain restrictions, but these shall only be such as are provided by law and are necessary:

   - For respect of the rights or reputations of others;

   - For the protection of national security or of public order (order public), or of public health or morals.

Article 20

... 2. Any advocacy of national, racial or religious hatred that constitutes incitement to discrimination, hostility or violence shall be prohibited by law.

The European Convention on Human Rights (ECHR), in its Articles 9 and 10 respectively, contains similar provisions to those in ICCPR Articles 18 and 19. It has no explicit equivalent to ICCPR Article 20. Specific cases referred to below relate to those of the ECtHR.

So what do these treaties offer, beyond confirmation that people should be free to speak and believe as they wish?

They set out a clear legal basis for obligations of States, and entitlements of individuals. In particular, they provide a framework for resolving tensions between freedom of speech and religion/belief that can arise in specific cases. They do so particularly through their limitations clauses.

Limitations? Surely free speech is free speech?

No. Freedom of expression as set out in Article 19 of the ICCPR and Article 10 of the ECHR expressly states that the exercise of the right to freedom of expression carries with it special duties and responsibilities. For this reason specific limitations are permitted, including when necessary for the protection of the rights of others. For example, freedom of speech doesn't give you the right to defame people. Nor is there is there an absolute right to insult religious believers or even their beliefs. Let alone threaten violence against them.

But what about critiquing religious doctrines?

The grounds for limiting both expression and manifestations of religion or belief are carefully drawn. They can only be imposed as prescribed by law, and as are necessary to protect the rights of others and public safety, etc.. And no limitations can be placed on individuals' right to think or believe (the 'forum internum'). The right to critique and challenge religious and other doctrines helps protect non-believers, people whose beliefs are branded 'heretic' by the mainstream, and believers themselves, of all religions and beliefs. Most if not all religions, after all, make claims on the veracity of at least some other faiths. The importance of this is recognised by the ECtHR and the Human Rights Committee, which are careful to ensure that restrictions on freedom of expression are carefully imposed in accordance with the exceptions provided for in the Conventions.

Can I provoke? Can I be offensive?

That depends – partly on what you say, how you say it, and on the effects that you produce. But also on where in the world you say it. States are afforded a margin of appreciation to decide whether and how to protect religious convictions and beliefs: in other words they have space for manoeuvre for deciding how to fulfil their obligations under human rights treaties. For example, a State can stop you showing on its territory a film which gratuitously offends religious sensibilities (cf. Otto-Preminger Institut v. Austria, Wingrove v. UK. Both, incidentally, about anti-Christianity films) or stop you publishing a passage in a book that constitutes an abusive attack on the Prophet of Islam. But whether a restriction is permissible will very much depend on the circumstances of the case and the situation in the country concerned. And in any case, any restriction must comply with the relevant limitations. Importantly, a State does not have to prohibit speech that is merely provocative or offensive about a religion.

The international human rights framework also distinguishes between speech that is offensive about religion and that which is offensive about race. Publicly criticising the value of a religious or other belief system may legitimately stimulate public debate ('Does God exist?', etc.). Whereas doing the same to a racial or ethnic group per se is not considered acceptable, not least as such criticism tends generally to be founded on the criticiser's perceived racial superiority over the group concerned.

Really? States can allow their citizens to say whatever they like about religions and believers?

Not quite. In addition to the restrictions on the freedom of expression in Article 19(3), Article 20 of the ICCPR requires States to prohibit 'advocacy of ... religious hatred that constitutes incitement to discrimination, hostility or violence'. But the threshold for expression to constitute such advocacy of religious hatred is high. Being offensive or provocative doesn't necessarily reach that threshold: it depends on the specifics of the case at hand. The degree of the hatred, the effects it generates, and the intent of its originator or distributor are all relevant, amongst other factors. The US, moreover, has a reservation on ICCPR, that 'Article 20 does not authorize or require legislation or other action by the United States that would restrict the right of free speech and association protected by the Constitution and laws of the United States'.

And what about in the UK?

The UK Racial and Religious Hatred Act 2006 makes it an offence for a person to use 'threatening words or behaviour, or display any written material which is threatening, ... if he intends thereby to stir up religious hatred'. Religious hatred being defined as 'hatred against a group of persons defined by reference to religious belief or lack of religious belief'. Similar provisions apply to publishing or distributing written materials or recordings. The Act is explicit, though, that:

'Nothing in this Part shall be read or given effect in a way which prohibits or restricts discussion, criticism or expressions of antipathy, dislike, ridicule, insult or abuse of particular religions or the beliefs or practices of their adherents, or of any other belief system or the beliefs or practices of its adherents, or proselytising or urging adherents of a different religion or belief system to cease practising their religion or belief system'.

The focus, therefore, is to protect believers rather than beliefs themselves.

24 March 2014

⇨ The above information is reprinted with kind permission from the Foreign & Commonwealth Office. Please visit www.gov.uk for further information.

Freedom of religion – universal right or matter of national security?

By Dr Erin Wilson (Twitter: @ek_wilson)

The extent to which Freedom of Religion and Belief (FoRB) should be promoted and protected as a foreign policy goal is becoming an increasing focus across numerous industrialised countries. While it has long been a priority for the US, the UK and the EU have also recently increased their efforts to place more emphasis on this right in their engagements abroad.[i] Yet this new found enthusiasm for FoRB is arguably being undermined by concurrent developments in the domestic public spheres of these countries.

The murder of Lee Rigby in the UK in 2013, the *Charlie Hebdo* attacks in Paris earlier this year, and the Copenhagen café shooting that has occurred only in the last few days, have all contributed to renewed fears of public displays and professions of religious belief, with governments being called on to implement even more strict regulations around the visibility of religion in the public sphere, both online and offline.[ii]

What are we to think when a government seeks to promote greater freedom of religion and belief in other countries while at the same time restricting freedom of religion and belief within their own borders? Such competing tendencies seem counter-intuitive and counter-productive. Surely, if FoRB really is the same universal right for everyone the world over, our commitment to it should be the same, regardless of whether we are considering the situation in our own country or whether we are looking elsewhere? In theory, yes, but in reality this is far from the case.

A key factor affecting government approaches to FoRB in domestic and foreign policies is that, in the post 9/11 and Global War on Terror context, anything related to 'religion', including FoRB, has become inextricably bound up with 'national security'. The link between 'religion' and 'security' is by no means a new development. Security and secularisation have arguably been bound together through the common assumption that the modern nation-state emerged as a response to the so-called 'Wars of Religion' of the sixteenth century. [iii] In this narrative, religion, we are told, is inherently dangerous, violent and irrational, leading to insecurity and chaos when it is not controlled by a secular state. This definition of religion creates the necessary justification for privatising it and excluding it from the public sphere through government imposed measures and controls.[iv] This is the secular logic that underpins the arrangement of religion's relationship with politics within the internal, domestic public spheres of most industrialised, so-called 'Western' countries. At the same time, however, since the late 1990s, and especially since the events of 9/11, the promotion of FoRB has become a central pillar of US and increasingly UK and EU foreign policy, underpinned in part by the belief that greater religious freedom abroad will contribute to increased security at home.

In both domestic and foreign policy, state intervention with regard to Freedom of Religion is justified in part in terms of national security. Making FoRB part of foreign policy efforts inevitably means that it is inextricably bound up with the goals and priorities of the nation-state, and given priority only insofar as it supports the broader security aims and goals of the state. As such, it is little wonder that efforts to promote FoRB abroad are often greeted with skepticism and cynicism, as a 'cover' for renewed imperial efforts by 'the West' and/or for the promotion of Christianity. Until FoRB is delinked from national security and until there is consistency across domestic and foreign policies on these issues, its status as a universal right, rather than a tool of national security agendas, will always remain in question.

[i] http://www.publications.parliament.uk/pa/cm201415/cmselect/cmfaff/551/55111.htm http://eeas.europa.eu/delegations/un_geneva/press_corner/all_news/news/2013/20131126_forb_en.htm

[ii] http://www.nytimes.com/2015/01/16/opinion/after-paris-attacks-wrong-responses-to-charlie-hebdo.html?_r=0 This is only the latest in a series of measures taken by some governments in the EU to restrict the public display of religious symbols and the presence of religious argumentation and profession in public debates, the most severe of which is arguably the 2004 ban on religious symbols in France.

[iii] Mavelli, L. 2011.'Security and Secularization in International Relations' *European Journal of International Relations* 18(1): 177-199

[iv] Wilson, E.K. 2012. After Secularism: Rethinking Religion in Global Politics. Basingstoke: Palgrave Macmillan.

17 February 2015

⇨ The above information is reprinted with kind permission from Westminster Faith Debates. Please visit www.faithdebates.org.uk for further information.

State hostility towards religion on the increase around the world

The number of states hostile to Christians up to 110, according to new figures.

State hostility towards religion is on the increase in most of the world's 198 nations, according to a new study by the Pew Research Center.

The share of countries with a high or very high level of social hostilities involving religion reached a six-year peak in 2012, the study said. The share of countries with a high or very high level of government restrictions on religion, however, remained stable.

This is the fifth time the Pew Research Center has reported on religious restrictions around the globe. The report was issued in advance of the US observance of Religious Freedom Day, 16 January.

The number of nations showing hostilities toward Christians rose from 106 to 110, according to the study. Christians have been the subject of religious hostility in more nations than any other group. But those countries showing hostilities toward Muslims jumped from 101 to 109 in 2012.

In fact, hostilities toward Jews, Hindus, Buddhists and folk religionists were all up from 2011 levels. The only group recording a decrease were 'others,' which includes Sikhs, Baha'is, Zoroastrians and other groups.

In overall changes taking into account both social hostilities and government restrictions, 61 pe rcent of nations recorded an increase, 29 per cent recorded a decrease and 10 per cent had no change.

On a scale of 0 to 10, 20 nations were given a score of at least 7.2, indicating very high social hostilities on religion, up from 14 in 2011. Pakistan once again topped the list. New countries joining the list were Syria, Lebanon, Sri Lanka, Bangladesh, Thailand and Myanmar.

In the case of government restrictions, the number of countries given a score of 6.6 or higher on a zero-to-ten scale indicating very high restrictions increased from 20 in 2011 to 24 in 2012.

Egypt led both years. New to the list are Azerbaijan, Tajikistan, Morocco, Iraq and Kazakhstan; Yemen dropped off the list.

'Overall, across the six years of this study, religious groups were harassed in a total of 185 countries at one time or another,' the study said. 'Members of the world's two largest religious groups – Christians and Muslims, who together comprise more than half of the global population – were harassed in the largest number of countries, 151 and 135, respectively.'

On social hostilities involving religion, the Middle East-North Africa region had a score of 6.4, more than twice that of the next-most-hostile region. The Americas had the lowest score, at 0.4.

The Pew study cited the August 2012 shooting at a Sikh temple in Wisconsin that left six worshippers dead and three others wounded as an incidence of 'religion-related terrorist violence.' The report said episodes took place in about 20 per cent of all countries in 2012, more than double the nine per cent figure of 2007.

The Middle East-North Africa region also had the highest regional score of government restrictions toward religion, at 6.2. The Americas were given the best score here, too, at 1.5.

The US received its third straight year of 'moderate' for both government restrictions on religion and social hostilities toward religion. Pew does not issue scores for individual countries, it said, 'because there are numerous tie scores and the differences between the scores of countries that are close to each other on this table are not necessarily meaningful'.

'None of the 25 most populous countries had low social hostilities involving religion in 2012,' the report said, while only five – Brazil, South Africa, the Philippines, Japan and the Democratic Republic of the Congo –

had low government restrictions on religion.

Countries whose score increased by at least one full point on Pew's 'social hostilities index' were Afghanistan, Somalia, the Palestinian territories, Syria, Kenya, Lebanon, Bangladesh, Thailand, Myanmar, Mali, Tunisia, Kosovo, Mexico, Greece, Algeria, France, Georgia, Italy, Vietnam, Turkey, Libya, Bahrain, Guinea, Ghana, Tuvalu, The Netherlands, China, Angola, Poland, Belgium, Zambia, Samoa, South Sudan, Comoros, Madagascar, Malawi, Slovenia, Ireland and Mozambique.

Nations that gained at least a full point on Pew's 'government restrictions index' were Tajikistan, Morocco, Iraq, Kazakhstan, Turkey, Bulgaria, Rwanda, Djibouti, Austria, Tuvalu, Iceland, Zambia, Hungary and Montenegro.

To make its determinations, Pew used 18 widely cited, publicly available sources of information, including reports by the State Department, the U.S. Commission on International Religious Freedom, the UN Special Rapporteur on Freedom of Religion or Belief, the Council of the European Union, the United Kingdom's Foreign & Commonwealth Office, Human Rights Watch, the International Crisis Group, Freedom House and Amnesty International.

16 January 2014

⇨ The above information is reprinted with kind permission from the *Catholic Herald*. Please visit www.catholicherald.co.uk for further information.

Creative and academic freedom under threat from religious intolerance in India

An article from The Conversation.

By Meena Vari

THE CONVERSATION

When asked what made him such a prolific painter, even at the age of 91, MF Hussain, known as the Indian Picasso, said it was three things: 'not worrying about critics and fundamentalists, working every day, and never wearing shoes.' The great painter went into self-imposed exile after threats from Hindu fundamentalists angry at his paintings of nude gods. He died in 2011 with an unfulfilled wish to come back to his home country, even if it was just for one afternoon.

From the publication of books, paintings and cartoons to ideas expressed on Facebook, public life for artists in India is tied up with censorship and threats of legal action. There was a time as Indians when we were proud of our values of pluralism and tolerance; now that is under attack along with academic freedom of expression.

'For a country that takes great pride in its democracy and history of free speech, the present situation is troubling,' Nilanjana Roy, a columnist and literary critic, said. 'Especially in the creative sphere, the last two decades have been progressively intolerant.'

Religion and communal sentiments are often invoked in today's censorship battles, although many of the underlying reasons for the attacks seem selfish, rather than stemming from a genuine interest for society.

In December 2014, Anand Patwardhan's 1992 documentary film *Ram Ke Naam* was supposed to screen at the Indian Law Society college in Pune. The film, about the politics of religion that drove the demolition of the Babri Masjid mosque in Ayodhya, is one of India's most significant socio-political documentaries.

However, the screening was called off after the college received threats. Another documentary maker, Sanjay Kak, whose 2007 film *Jashn-e-Azadi* is critical of the army's role in Kashmir, has also seen attacks on venues that planned to show his film.

Curricula under pressure

In academia, one of the biggest controversies in recent years centred around an essay, *Three Hundred Ramayanas: Five Examples and Three Thoughts on Translations*, by well-known historian A K Ramanujan about different versions of the Ramayana, a religious text.

The essay was included in the University of Delhi's BA History syllabus in 2006 to highlight the

fact that there are Dalit, feminist, and other popular versions of the text in other Asian countries. One of the students made a complaint and a right-wing political party took up the issue, which led to a petition filed at the Delhi Supreme Court to drop the essay.

Even though three of the four members of the committee established by the court recommended the continuation of the essay as part of the syllabus, the university's academic council decided to abandon it.

Some artists have made the decision to bow out of public life because of the attacks on their work. In January, Perumal Murugan, a well-known novelist in the Tamil language, announced on Facebook that he was giving up writing:

Perumal Murugan, the writer, is dead. As he is no God, he is not going to resurrect himself. He has no faith in rebirth. As an ordinary teacher, he will live as P Murugan. Leave him alone.

This came after virulent protests by Hindu and local caste-based groups over his novel, *Madhorubhagan*. They complained the novel denigrated Hindu deities and women. The protests started four years after it was published in Tamil, but Murugan has said he believes it was the English translation, *One Part Woman*, published at the end of 2014 that started the uproar.

The right to freedom is one of the fundamental rights in the Indian constitution that also includes the freedom of speech and expression. This means, in principle, there is creative freedom. But the lines are blurred as to whether Indians have the privilege to use religion

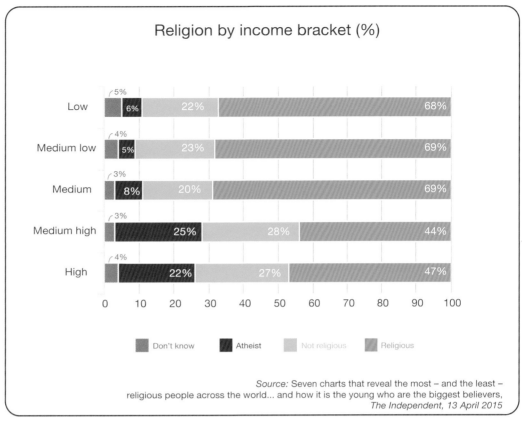

Religion by income bracket (%)

	Don't know	Atheist	Not religious	Religious
Low	5%	6%	22%	68%
Medium low	4%	5%	23%	69%
Medium	3%	8%	20%	69%
Medium high	3%	25%	28%	44%
High	4%	22%	27%	47%

Source: Seven charts that reveal the most – and the least – religious people across the world... and how it is the young who are the biggest believers, The Independent, 13 April 2015

as a context, resource or reference point in their creative outputs.

Creative practitioners – writers, artists or the filmmakers – are typically not interested in exploring the faith, philosophy or the devotion attached to religion. They use the stories, rituals, customs and history. For example, in his novel, Murugan used folklore, which had originated as part of the Hindu chariot festival, about a mating ritual where one day a year there can be consensual sex between any man and woman.

The author has explained there is no historical evidence for the ritual, which was part of the oral stories that had been passed down through the generations. He had used this aspect in his novel not to create religious tensions, but to highlight the discriminatory powers of the caste system and the situation for women.

No logical thinking

Personally, I believe that being Indian means being confident in our roots. This is not just about what language you speak or religion you practise, but the entire social and cultural set-up. My family comes from Kerala, so my mother tongue

is Malayalam, but I was born in Uttar Pradesh, so the first language I spoke is Hindi and English became my working language. I was born into a Catholic family and married a Hindu. I always thought when I grew up things would be very different. Yet it is quite paradoxical that in this age and era, we stop to think logically when it comes to religion.

Indians are happy to borrow, buy or develop progressive ideas in order to grow the economy faster. Wider roads, new shopping malls and buildings are coming up every day; the old cities are being torn down to make way for new ones. Modernity is slowly moving in; but when it comes to freedom to speak about religion, reason has taken a back seat.

1 July 2015

⇨ The above information is reprinted with kind permission from *The Conversation*. Please visit www.theconversation.com for further information.

Key facts

⇨ According to the 2011 UK Census, those of no religion are the second largest belief group, about three and a half times as many as all the non-Christian religions put together – at 26.13% of the population. (page 1)

⇨ 16,038,229 people said they had 'no religion' with a further 4,406,032 (7.18%) not stating a religion. (page 1)

⇨ 58.81% described their religion as Christian and 7.88% as some non-Christian religion. This represented a massive change from the 2001 Census, where 15.5% of the population recorded having no religion, and 72% of the population reported being Christian. (page 1)

⇨ In the UK, the percentage of the population which describes itself as belonging to no religion has risen from 31.4% to 50.6% between 1983 and 2013 according to the British Social Attitudes Survey's 31st report issued in 2014. Among people aged between 15 and 24, the incidence of religious affiliation is only 30.7%. It is only amongst the over-55s that the majority of respondents are religious. (page 1)

⇨ The 2014 British Social Attitudes Survey found that 58.4% of the population never attend religious services while only 13.1% of people report going to a religious service once a week or more. (page 2)

⇨ In a 2007 survey conducted by YouGov on behalf of the broadcaster and writer John Humphries, 42% of the participants believed religion had a harmful effect. (page 2)

⇨ A 2012 YouGov poll found that 58% of Britons do not believe that bishops should sit in the House of Lords. 65% of people think that Bishops are out of touch with public opinion. (page 4)

⇨ A sixth (17%) of people think that 'miracles are the result of God or a higher power intervening in nature', whereas nearly a third (30%) take the opposite view, namely that 'miracles don't exist – they are simply examples of coincidence or luck'. (page 5)

⇨ 13% of people say they prayed 'daily or more often', 8% say they prayed a few times a week and 34% said they prayed occasionally. Nearly a half, or 45%, of people say they never prayed. (page 5)

⇨ In the US, nearly six in ten people, 56 per cent, said they were religious. One third said they were not religious and just six per cent were convinced atheists. (page 7)

⇨ A poll has shown Thailand to be the most religious country globally with more than nine in ten people being religious. More than nine in ten people said they were religious also in Armenia, Bangladesh, Georgia and Morocco. (page 7)

⇨ Muslims in Britain constitute only 5% of the British population. (page 12)

⇨ Whereas 72% of those born before 1945 would regard themselves as belonging to a religion, the figure is 51% for Baby Boomers, 40% for Generation X and 38% for Generation Y. (page 18)

⇨ If current trends continue, by 2050:

  • The number of Muslims will nearly equal the number of Christians around the world.

  • Atheists, agnostics and other people who do not affiliate with any religion – though increasing in countries such as the US and France – will make up a declining share of the world's total population.

  • The global Buddhist population will be about the same size it was in 2010, while the Hindu and Jewish populations will be larger than they are today.

  • In Europe, Muslims will make up 10% of the overall population.

  • India will retain a Hindu majority but also will have the largest Muslim population of any country in the world, surpassing Indonesia. (page 21)

⇨ In Europe, the Muslim share of the population is expected to increase from 5.9% in 2010 to 10.2% in 2050. (page 23)

⇨ Of the 196 countries in the world, 81 countries – or 41 per cent – are identified as places where religious freedom is impaired (classified as 'high' or 'medium') or is in decline. (page 31)

⇨ Christians have been the subject of religious hostility in more nations than any other group. But those countries showing hostilities toward Muslims jumped from 101 to 109 in 2012. (page 37)

Agnosticism

An agnostic believes that it is impossible to know or prove whether there is a god. The term 'agnostic' is also used for those who are sceptical of the existence of a god, but do not firmly commit to atheism.

Atheism

Atheism refers to the firm belief that there is no god or divine power at work in the universe, and human beings are constrained to one life only, with no continued existence after death.

Buddhism

Buddhism began in Northern India over 2,500 years ago. It is based upon the teachings of the Buddha, who sought to free himself and others from suffering and discover enlightenment.

Burqa

A burqa is a garment originally introduced by the Taliban in Afghanistan. It completely covers a woman's body and face, providing only a grille through which to see. It is distinct from the more common niqab, which leaves a slit for the eyes. The hijab is by far the most common garment worn by Muslim women in the UK, however: a headscarf which does not cover the face.

Christianity

Christianity is the largest religion in the world. Christians follow the teachings of Jesus Christ, who they believe to be the son of God, as given in the Bible – however, there are many different denominations and sects, with varying beliefs and rituals. These include Catholicism, Orthodox Christianity and Protestantism (which incorporates other groups such as the Methodists, the Baptists and the Church of England).

Faith school

A faith school is subject to the national curriculum, but is affiliated to a particular religious faith or denomination.

Faith-based abuse

Child abuse or other crimes that can be linked to faith, religion or belief.

Free school

Free schools the same freedoms and flexibilities as academies, but they do not normally replace an existing school. Free schools may be set up by a wide range of proposers – including charities, universities, businesses, educational groups, teachers and groups of parents.

Hinduism

Hinduism is an ancient Indian religion with no precise traceable beginning or single founder. Its central belief is in the existence of a natural order, a balanced way of living: physically, socially, ethically and spiritually.

Humanism

Humanism is a non-religious philosophy whose adherents propound an approach to life based on liberal human values and reason. Humanists believe that we do not need religious guidance in order to make moral choices. They believe that as this life is the only life we have, it is important to live it in an ethical and fulfilling way.

Islam

Islam is the second largest faith group in the UK today – 2.8% of the UK population were Muslims in 2001, according to the last census. Muslims believe in the word of Allah (God) as set out in their holy book, the Quran, by the prophet Muhammad in Arabia 1,300 years ago. Islam is a way of life, and followers must observe strict rules regarding diet, lifestyle and worship.

Islamophobia

An extreme fear and hatred of Islam and people who follow the Islam faith, otherwise known as Muslims. Since the 11 September 2001 terrorist attacks in New York and Washington and the 7/7 London bombings (7 July 2005), there have been a lot of strong, controversial debates surrounding Muslims and Islam. This has provoked unfair stereotyping of Muslims as people associate their faith with extreme terrorist actions.

Judaism

Judaism dates back over 4,000 years, originating in the Middle East. The Jewish faith believes in one God who has revealed His will for them through their holy book, the Torah.

Religion

The word religion comes from the *Latin religio*, which means 'duty'. It can be defined as a set of beliefs, rituals and values centred around faith in a supernatural power at work in the universe. Major world religions followed in the UK today include Christianity, Islam, Hinduism, Sikhism, Judaism and Buddhism.

Secularism

The National Secular Society describes secularism as 'a principle that involves two basic propositions. The first is the strict separation of the state from religious institutions. The second is that people of different religions and beliefs are equal before the law'.

Sikhism

The Sikh tradition began in the Punjab region over 500 years ago. It was founded by Guru Nanak, the first teacher of the faith. Sikhs believe in one God, before whom everyone is equal. A good life is lived as part of a community, by living honestly and caring for others.

Assignments

Brainstorming

⇨ In small groups, discuss what you know about faith and religion. Consider the following:

- What are some of the different world religions?

- What religions are prevalent in the UK?

Research

⇨ Read the article *The spirit of things unseen: belief in post-religious Britain* on page four and identify some of the key questions asked. Using these questions, conduct your own survey amongst friends, family and class-mates then write a summary of your findings. You could also include graphs to illustrate your summary.

⇨ Read the article *Ramadan fasting: modern opposition to age-old rules* on page 14 and do some research to find out about other religious traditions that might need to be adapted to a more modern way of life. Share your findings with your class.

⇨ In pairs, research religious education and the law in the UK to find out what schools are required to teach. Write notes and feedback to your class.

⇨ Choose one of the following faiths and find out more about its origins, what its members believe and how they worship: Christianity/Islam/Hinduism/Sikhism/Judaism/Buddhism/another faith of your choice (if you belong to one of these faiths, choose one other than your own to research). Write a summary of your findings.

Design

⇨ Read the article *Religion and belief: some surveys and statistics* on page one and create a poster that demonstrates at least ten key statistics.

⇨ Choose one of the articles in this book and create an illustration to highlight the key themes/messages of your chosen article.

⇨ In small groups, design a campaign that will attract young people back to the Church of England. Your campaign could be based in print (e.g. posters and leaflets) or digitally (e.g. social media and websites).

⇨ Create a leaflet that highlights employees' religious rights in the work place.

Oral

⇨ Stage a class debate centred around the question: 'Should the UK adopt the French approach to religion and become a secularist state?' Half of you should argue 'Yes' and the other half should argue 'No'.

⇨ In pairs, discuss why soldiers today still turn to the Bible and prayer while on the front line.

⇨ Choose one of the illustrations in this book and, in pairs, discuss why the artist chose to depict the themes they did.

⇨ Choose a religion and create a PowerPoint presentation that explores its key beliefs and traditions.

Reading/writing

⇨ Read the article *Two thirds of people worldwide are religious (but less than one third of Brits)* on page seven and rank the countries mentioned in order of how religious their population is. Choose one of the countries from your list and conduct further research to identify the key religions in each of these countries. Share your findings with your class.

⇨ Write an article or blog about Britain's 'atheist church' the Sunday Assembly.

⇨ Write definitions of the terms 'faith' and 'religion' then compare your definitions with a friend's.

⇨ Visit the British Humanist Association website – www.humanism.org.uk – and find out more about this non-religious life philosophy. What do humanists believe? By what principles do they live their lives? What areas does the BHA currently campaign in? Prepare a short presentation about humanism and deliver it to your class.

⇨ Over the course of a week, read at least three newspapers (either in print or online) and identify any articles that discuss faith or religion – noting their titles and themes. At the end of the week, compare the articles you have looked at and write one-paragraph answers to the following questions:

- Does any one faith in particular receive more coverage than others?

- Is the press coverage mainly positive or negative?

- Does the positivity of the coverage differ depending on which faith the article is written about?

- What are the key issues of the week?

Acknowledgements

The publisher is grateful for permission to reproduce the material in this book. While every care has been taken to trace and acknowledge copyright, the publisher tenders its apology for any accidental infringement or where copyright has proved untraceable. The publisher would be pleased to come to a suitable arrangement in any such case with the rightful owner.

Images

Pages 8, 12 and 33: iStock, page 7 © Aaron Burden, page 11 © U.S Army Africa, page 22 © Stefan Kunze, page 24 © Omer Unlu, page 28: SXC, page 38 © Arlan Zwegers.

Illustrations

Don Hatcher: pages 10 & 35. Simon Kneebone: pages 4 & 29. Angelo Madrid: pages 16 & 31.

Additional acknowledgements

Editorial on behalf of Independence Educational Publishers by Cara Acred.

With thanks to the Independence team: Mary Chapman, Sandra Dennis, Christina Hughes, Jackie Staines and Jan Sunderland.

Cara Acred

Cambridge

September 2015